JOËLLE TH
UNDER $20
WINE GUIDE

To my sisters Susan and Jacqui,
who love wine, in moderation

First published in 2003 by New Holland Publishers (NZ) Ltd

Auckland • Sydney • London • Cape Town
218 Lake Road, Northcote, Auckland, New Zealand
14 Aquatic Drive, Frenchs Forest, NSW 2086, Australia
86–88 Edgware Road, London W2 2EA, United Kingdom
80 McKenzie Street, Cape Town 8001, South Africa

www.newhollandpublishers.com

Copyright © 2003 in text: Joëlle Thomson
Copyright © 2003 New Holland Publishers (NZ) Ltd

ISBN: 1 86966 031 5

Publishing manager: Renée Lang
Cover photograph: Andrew Coffey
Hair and make-up by Lauren Gunn for Stephen Marr Hair Design
Clothes by Kate Sylvester
Editor: Barbara Nielsen/Stylus Publishing Services Ltd
Typesetting: Julie McDermid/Punaromia

THE LOCATION ... for this year's cover photograph was
Caro's Wine,
124 Ponsonby Road, Auckland

A catalogue record for this book is available from the
National Library of New Zealand

10 9 8 7 6 5 4 3 2 1

Printed by McPherson's Printing Group, Australia

All rights reserved. No part of this publication may be reproduced,
stored in a retrieval system, or transmitted in any form or by any means,
electronic, mechanical, photocopying, recording or otherwise, without
the prior permission of the publishers and copyright holders.

Every effort has been made to ensure that all the information, including retail prices, stated in this book was correct at the time of publication. The author and publishers expressly disclaim all liability to any person or persons arising directly or indirectly from the use of, or for any errors or omissions in, the information in this book.

JOËLLE THOMSON'S
UNDER $20
WINE GUIDE
2003/2004 EDITION

ABOUT THE AUTHOR

Joëlle Thomson's first paid writing job was reporting on school news, local artists and shipping timetables at the *Bay of Plenty Times* in Tauranga, in 1991. This was followed by an underpaid reporting stint at the short-lived UHF television's Channel 58 in Dunedin, and then a job as copywriter for the television game show, *The Price is Right*. When the show ended less than six months into its life, Joëlle left New Zealand's media scene to work in bars, restaurants and nightclubs in London, Edinburgh and the Shetland Islands, indulging her passion for wine by drinking it every day.

In 1994 Joëlle returned to Wellington, New Zealand, where she worked at *Capital Times Arts Weekly* for four years. She then became features editor for *FQ Entertaining* magazine and later worked on *SHE*, *Cleo*, *Australian Women's Weekly*, *New Zealand Home & Entertaining* and *Your Home & Garden* as well as writing weekly wine columns for the *Havelock North Village Press*, the *Christchurch Press* and the *Dominion*.

Joëlle is now the wine columnist for New Zealand's largest daily newspaper, the *New Zealand Herald*, and Television New Zealand's website nzoom.com

In 2002 *Joëlle Thomson's Under $20 Wine Guide* won Best Wine Guide at the World Cookbook Awards in France.

She co-wrote the New Zealand section for the *Global Encyclopedia of Wine* (2000) and is a member of the British-based Circle of Wine Writers. Joëlle has been a wine and food judge in New Zealand and Australia. She lives in Auckland, New Zealand.

ALSO BY JOËLLE THOMSON
- *Joëlle Thomson's Under $15 Wine Guide (1999, 2000, 2001, 2002)*
- *101 Wine Tips*
- *Weekends for Wine Lovers in the North Island*

CONTENTS

Introduction	7
Joëlle Thomson's wine awards 2003	10
Wines of the year	12
Guide to our guide	14
How wines were tasted	17
Wine stuff you need to know	18

WHITE WINES

Breidecker	24
Chardonnay	25
Chenin blanc	61
Gewürztraminer	64
Müller-thurgau	69
Other white wines and branded whites	71
Pinot gris	76
Riesling	82
Sauvignon blanc	101
Sémillon and sémillon-predominant white blends	123
Viognier	126

ROSÉ

128

RED WINES

Beaujolais and Gamay	134
Cabernet sauvignon, cabernet franc and cabernet-dominant red blends	137
Côtes-du-Rhône	168
Grenache	171
Malbec	175
Merlot and merlot-dominant reds	178
Other red blends and branded red wines	194
Pinotage	206
Pinot noir	209
Sangiovese	215
Shiraz and syrah	216

BUBBLIES 236

SWEET TREATS 251

FORTIFIEDS

Sherry and sherry-styled fortified wines	256
Port, Marsala and port look-alikes, and fortified wines	259

Acknowledgements 264

> 'Compromises are for relationships, not for wine.'
>
> SIR ROBERT SCOTT CAYWOOD

INTRODUCTION

New Zealanders are a curious bunch. We drink more shiraz, merlot, pinot noir, chardonnay, riesling and pinot gris than we did a year ago but we are not drinking more wine.

Our annual wine consumption per head of population has been static at around 17 litres per head each year for at least half a decade. About eight litres of that 17 consists of locally produced wine, while the rest comes from overseas. One could easily surmise that we are becoming more health-conscious but our ever-expanding waistlines have been well documented.

Even more curiously, while New Zealanders are moving away from cask wines and cheap bottled wines, we are spending less per bottle of wine than we did a year ago. Bottles of wine costing $15–20, once the fastest growing category, have now lost pace to $11–15 bottles of wine. The temporary blip might be because, at the time of writing, our first decent summer in years had finally arrived and some of us were also reaching for tall glasses of G&T with ice and a slice as often as a refreshing glass of white wine, but Montana Wines international sales manager Ian Hall prefers to see it as something even less threatening to wine sales than such a seasonal variation.

'The downward trend over the last few months is driven by aggressive retail,' he says, adding that the trend will swing back to the $15–20 category this year. 'In the over-$20 category we have been growing at a very fast rate – 32 percent, in supermarkets over the last year – so we as a company are focusing on premium wines in all sectors of the market, which means we put more emphasis for quality wine making and marketing on the $15–20 category than anything under that.'

As a company, Montana Wines is New Zealand's largest wine producer and also a large importer of wines from Australia, Italy and France, so that emphasis is significant.

Just how we can be consuming more of most types of wine but no more wine overall seems perplexing until you realise that New Zealanders are generally spending more per bottle of wine, from $6 upwards.

Sales of last year's edition of *Joëlle Thomson's Under $20 Wine Guide* grew slightly from the previous *Under $15 Wine Guide*, which also testifies to a national interest in the quality of wine rather than the quantity.

The trend in our drinking habits is towards better quality, more flavour, more bang for your buck. And that is where this book comes in. There are only two criteria a wine must have to make it into this guide: it has to cost less than $20 and it has to be available in New Zealand – not necessarily available in large quantities but able to be purchased somewhere in the country.

The aim of the guide is to ferret out the good, the bad and the rest and rate all of them with an easy-to-follow star system. You can read the comments if you like but it is the star rating that holds most credence in this guide, which features wine from all over the world.

Perhaps the most curious thing about New Zealanders' wine-drinking habits is that the fastest growth in wine consumption in this country is in sparkling wine. From November 2002 to January 2003, sparkling wine costing $11–15 a bottle grew by 66 percent in volume, driven by sales of the appealing coloured, strawberry-flavoured Lindauer Fraise produced by Montana Wines.

Ian Hall says that Fraise has grown without taking market shares off other wine brands or companies. 'We are trying to grow the wine market, that is our biggest aim.'

And given the teenage penchant for ready-to drink, premixed

spirits, anything that can grow a safer, lower-alcohol drink gets a big thumbs up from me. This year's book features surprise good-value buys across the market from less than $10 up to $19.95, making it possible for everybody to afford a taste sensation.

I hope you enjoy this year's guide and find the growth in wine styles and quality as fascinating and tasty as I have.

TALK TO ME
If you have any feedback, suggestions or comments on the evolution of *Joëlle Thomson's Under $20 Wine Guide*, let me and my publishers know.

Tell us via email: jthomson@xtra.co.nz or fax: (09) 376 8093.

I look forward to hearing from you.

Joëlle Thomson

JOËLLE THOMSON'S WINE AWARDS 2003

This year the choice of top wine was trickier than ever. The 2001 Carchelo Jumilla is so sweet and friendly in style that it is easy to imagine the wine is a simple soft quaffer, end of story. Nothing could be further from the truth. This wine has improved hands down year after year and deserves its position in 2003 as Wine of the Year.

All four contenders for Wine of the Year in the 2003/2004 edition of *Joëlle Thomson's Under $20 Wine Guide* were reds, but that is where their similarities end. The countries they came from, Spain, New Zealand, Italy and Chile, were represented by completely different wine styles, making it a case of judging apples with pears, oranges and feijoas. They were tasted in Riedel and Spiegelau wine glasses and, after much deliberation, retasting (blind) and consideration, the best wine was chosen.

WINE OF THE YEAR
★★★★ $14-16
2001 Carchelo Jumilla
The immediate impression in every mouthful of this wine is one of softness. All that soft, juicy texture comes from the monastrell (aka mourvedre) and the merlot grapes in the blend. The tempranillo adds body and oomph to this flavourful, deceptively gutsy, raspberry-tasting red. It is made by Vinedos Agapito Rico in Spain and, at $14–16, this is exceptional value for money.

🍷 *Specialist wine stores or contact Eurowine, phone (09) 636 4045.*

BEST-VALUE WINE OF THE YEAR
★★★½ $12-13 (1.5 litres cost just $18-20)
2001 Fiorile Rosso Sicilia
This Sicilian red is another incredibly good-value-for-money wine. It is soft, smooth and overridingly spicy as well fruit driven with light,

fresh fruit flavours and a lingering finish. Too easy to drink, very easy to afford but the good news is that its alcohol levels are average rather than high, so you can avoid red wine headaches.

🍷 *Specialist wine stores or contact importer Phil Clark at A Touch of Italy, phone (09) 273 3701, email: sales@touchofitaly.co.nz*

SPARKLING WINE OF THE YEAR
★★★½ **$15-16**
Lindauer Special Reserve

This is one of the best-value and best-tasting sparkling wines in the book this year, flavoursome in a way that implies pinot noir's cherry tastes and robust body. It has deliciously long lingering flavours and an extremely good-value price tag.

🍷 *Widely available.*

WINERY OF THE YEAR
Promessa

I loved the Promessa wines in this year's guide. Californian winemaker Mark Shannon and his marketing partner, Elvezia Sbalchiero, are together making some of the world's most exciting wines today. Exciting not because they bowl you over, as Shannon's personality does, but rather because their subtlety sneaks up and catches you by surprise. So it is with both the Promessa Negroamaro (one of Italy's indigenous grape varieties) and the softer Promessa Rosso Salento. Both wines are made from very old grapevines in Apuglia, southern Italy, where Shannon has adopted modern winemaking techniques to extract the most finesse from these smooth Italian reds. It's early days yet, but the flavour is already sensational and the potential is great. Check out the two wines: their details are in the 'Other Red Blends and Branded Red Wines' chapter, under 'Italy'.

WINES OF THE YEAR

 The 'star buy' symbol used throughout the book denotes the 'Wine of the Year' in each category.

CHARDONNAY
   2002 Matua Matheson Chardonnay $18-19 ★★★★

CHENIN BLANC
   2002 Collards Hawke's Bay Chenin Blanc $12-14 ★★★

GEWÜRZTRAMINER
   2002 Collards Hawke's Bay Gewürztraminer $15-17 ★★★★

MÜLLER-THURGAU
   2002 Corbans White Label Müller-Thurgau $8-9 ★★½

OTHER WHITE WINES OR BRANDED WHITE
   2001 Umani Ronchi Villa Bianchi Verdicchio $15-16 ★★★

PINOT GRIS
   2002 Bodega Lurton Pinot Gris $17-18 ★★★★

RIESLING
   2002 Esk Valley Hawke's Bay Riesling $19-20 ★★★★

SAUVIGNON BLANC
   2002 Wither Hills Marlborough Sauvignon Blanc $19-20 ★★★★

SÉMILLON
   2002 Glenguin The Old Broke Block Sémillon $19-20 ★★★★

VIOGNIER
   2002 Yalumba South Australia Y Viognier $16-17 ★★★½

ROSÉ
   2002 Kim Crawford Pansy $17-18 ★★★½

BEAUJOLAIS AND GAMAY
   2002 Woodthorpe Gamay Noir $19-20 ★★★½

CABERNET SAUVIGNON
   1999 Richmond Grove Coonawarra Limited Release Cabernet Sauvignon $19-20 ★★★★

CÔTES-DU-RHÔNE
  1999 Les Classes Côtes-du-Rhône Villages $14-15 ★★★½
GRENACHE
  2000 Domaine Saint-Pierre Corbières $15-16 ★★★½
MALBEC
  2000 Montes Reserve Malbec Oak Aged $19-20 ★★★½
MERLOT
  2001 Les Salices Merlot Vin de Pays D'Oc $17-18 ★★★½
OTHER RED BLENDS OR BRANDED RED
  2001 Carchelo Jumilla $14-15 ★★★★
PINOTAGE
  2001 Sanctuary Marlborough Pinotage/Pinot Noir $14-15 ★★★
PINOT NOIR
  2002 Shingle Peak Marlborough Pinot Noir $18-19 ★★★
SHIRAZ
  1999 Yalumba Barossa Shiraz $19-20 ★★★★
UNDER $10 BUBBLY
  Bernadino Spumante $7-8 ★★★½
$10-15 BUBBLY
  Jacob's Creek Chardonnay Pinot Noir Brut Cuvée $11-12 ★★★
$15-20 BUBBLY
  Lindauer Special Reserve $15-16 ★★★½
SWEET TREATS
  2002 Saints Gisborne Noble Sémillon $16-17 ★★★½
SHERRY
  Pykes Medium Sherry $11-12 ★★★
FORTIFIED WINE
  Pellegrino Dom De Marsala $17-18 ★★★
PORT
  Pykes Fine Tawny $19-20 ★★★

GUIDE TO OUR GUIDE

There are no funny symbols, tricky-to-work-out cellaring suggestions or any other finicky things to translate – just what it is, how much it costs, how good it is, what it tastes like and where to get it.

Take this entry as an example:

★★★ **2001 Robard & Butler Shiraz**
$10-11 Fresh and fruity but a little hard on the finish. Still it has robust fruit flavours, despite the oaky tannic finish. Good value at this amazing price, would stand up well to a rare steak.

 Widely available.

★★★ = three stars is a relatively high rating and means that this wine is worthy of a bronze medal.

$10-11 = the recommended retail price, provided by the winery that submitted the wine. This may vary from store to store but probably it will not exceed that which is stated.

2001 = the vintage, or year in which the grapes were harvested to make this wine. In some cases, for example most champagnes and sparkling wines, the wine is non-vintage. This is usually to achieve a consistent style at an affordable price.

Robard & Butler Shiraz = 'Robard & Butler' is the brand name of the wine, owned now by Montana Wines, which is the largest winery in New Zealand.

'Fresh and fruity but…' = my description of the wine based on tasting this wine and my tasting and knowledge of the shiraz wine style.

🍷 = 'where to buy' information, which has been supplied by the winery or distributor of the wine. It is not necessarily the only place to buy the wine, but it will provide you with an idea of where you can find it.

Wines in the guide are listed alphabetically in each chapter, with the exception of the 'Other White/Red Blends and Branded Whites/Reds' chapters, where the wines are grouped according to their country of origin.

THE STAR RATINGS

★	Avoid.
★½	Barely drinkable.
★★	Below average but drinkable.
★★½	Tastes good – nearly equivalent to a bronze medal-winning wine.
★★★	Fab value for money – bronze medal-winner equivalent.
★★★½	Excellent stuff with lots of flavour and great value at this price.
★★★★	Top notch, especially at this price, and silver medal standard.
★★★★½	Deliciously complex wine, outstanding value for money.
★★★★★	Extraordinarily good wine if it gets five stars at this price level, gold medal-worthy.

For this guide I have used the following star ratings, which are translated from the 20-point international wine judging system.

Score	Stars
13.5	★
14	★★
14.5-15	★★½
15.5-16	★★★
16.5	★★★½
17	★★★★
17.5-18	★★★★½
18.5-20	★★★★★

PRICE AND STOCKISTS DISCLAIMER

All prices stated in this guide are recommended retail prices supplied to the author at the time the book went to print. The wine stores, supermarkets and other retail outlets given here are not necessarily the only stockists of each wine listed.

The author regrets that it is not possible to list every single outlet that stocks the wine, since the size of this book prohibits that. All wines listed may also be purchased at the winery where they were made.

HOW WINES WERE TASTED

This year the tastings were held around the clock with a tasting glass, a laptop and two cats for company. Most of the time the room was brimming over with boxes of wine to be tasted but swift, long tastings held early in the morning and late in the evening managed to clear the decks for the next lot of wine to arrive via friendly couriers.

Tasting the wine is the most important part of the process of writing this book because it determines the quality and therefore the ratings of wines featured. It has been my preference to taste wine blind, with the identity of the wine concealed, but logistically this has proven to be in the too-hard basket for this book, working, as I do, as a one-person band, sending out invites for the tastings, opening all the boxes and letters, inputting information about each wine, tasting each one, and then rating it and writing a tasting note and description.

Experience has shown me that my palate becomes weary and less effective after about 50 wines, which has been the limit for me to taste at any one time for this book. Rather than taste 50 chardonnays and become worn out by similar styles and flavours, I have tasted two or three different styles of wine in a single sitting so that each style tastes like a fresh challenge.

The following wine books provide essential information and helpful reading if you want to learn more about wine tasting:
Hugh Johnson's How to Enjoy Your Wine by Hugh Johnson
The Sensational Liquid, a Guide to Wine Tasting by Malcolm Gluck
Discovering Wine by Joanna Simon
How to Match Food and Wine by Fiona Beckett
Wine by Hugh Johnson (now out of print but second-hand bookshops often yield a copy of this brilliant book)

WINE STUFF YOU NEED TO KNOW

THE STOPPER DEBATE
Screwcaps are the most radical thing to happen to wine in the last 100 years, according to Tim Finn, winemaker from Neudorf Vineyards in Nelson. It was August 2001 when screwcaps were being launched as an alternative to cork, and now, in 2003, about 20 percent of all New Zealand wine is sealed with a screwcap, ranging in price from the lowest wines in the market right up to some of the country's top chardonnays, rieslings, sauvignon blancs, pinot noirs, cabernet-based reds and merlots.

The country's third largest winery, Villa Maria, has converted to 100 percent screwcaps because, in the words of owner George Fistonich, he cares too much about quality to worry about tradition.

The traditional wine stopper has been used to seal bottles of wine for hundreds of years, with enough mysterious pomp and ceremony to sink a ship. Largely because of that pomp and ceremony, screwcap wine seals are polarising wine drinkers all over the world, except for those unhampered by tradition.

THE FACTS ABOUT CORK AND SCREWCAPS
Cork taint refers to the flavour of wine adversely affected by cork. This taint is caused by a mould called trichloranisole, or TCA for short. The level of TCA varies from cork to cork, which means the degree of cork taint varies from bottle to bottle and is unpredictable until a wine is opened.

At its most obvious, a cork-tainted wine takes on a musty smell like damp cardboard, mouldy wood or old wet shoes. The taste of the wine is also affected. If only marginally tainted, the wine will seem plain, dull and sometimes just tasteless. Cork taint is often more prevalent in composite cork made from relatively young cork trees, but it also occurs in top-grade cork.

The scewcap is made from an aluminium shell, the liner of

which consists of three layers. Directly in contact with the wine is a PVDC (polyvinylidene chloride) film, which is a high-grade, food-rated material. This is laminated to a very thin layer of tin, and these two surfaces provide a barrier to keep wine in and air out. They are then laminated to a wad of expanded foam, which sits on the glass of the bottle.

The other alternative to cork is plastic or other synthetic 'cork' closures, which have been shown to leak, allow wine to oxidise (unlike corks, they do not expand naturally in the bottle to slow the rate of oxidation) and also impart a flavour taint of their own after a period of time.

If you taste a wine that smells or tastes dusty or dirty, send it back. Good wine waiters and wine stores will replace corked wine, and if yours won't, vote with your feet.

The cork tree is an oak tree called *Quercus suber*, which grows in hot dry climates such as southern Portugal, Spain and France, northern Africa and Italy. Its unique feature is its soft outer bark, the first harvest of which can be taken only after 25 years and then can be used only to make agglomerate (particle-cork) products for floorings, shoes and insulation. Subsequent harvests can then be taken only at nine-year intervals, and the bark can be harvested only in fine weather, because in wind and rain it develops a natural glue, which adheres strongly to the tree trunk, acting as a defence against bad weather. Stripping the tree of its outer bark does not harm it, because the first layer of reproduction cork merges with the continuously developing virgin layer in the unpeeled part of the tree. Cork trees grow to be about 150–200 years old.

* To find out more about the New Zealand Screwcap Initiative, its rationale, modern screwcap technology and general information about wine stoppers, check out the New Zealand Screwcap Wine Seal Initiative's new website: www.screwcap.co.nz

WHERE AND HOW TO KEEP AND SERVE WINE

Even when it is for everyday drinking, wine needs to be treated with respect, and the following handy hints will ensure you get the most out of each bottle of wine.

- DO put half-consumed bottles of wine in the fridge with the cork (or rubber stopper – see below) firmly back in the bottle. This will maximise the wine's staying power by minimising the negative impact of oxidation on the wine.
- DO store full bottles of unopened wine on their sides. This keeps the cork moist and reduces the risk of the cork drying out, which increases the risk of oxidation.
- DO buy rubber stoppers that come with wine savers. Most kitchen and fine wine stores either sell them or can tell you where to get them. The vacuum pump is hardly worth using, since it barely removes any oxygen in the bottle, but the rubber stoppers are a far cleaner way of resealing half-full bottles that you don't drink at one sitting.
- DO buy a decent wine stopper so that you can reseal your wines in the cleanest, most effective way possible. Cork can impart dusty, dirty flavours to wine, especially if the opposite end is jammed back in a bottle, so opt for high quality, inert stoppers like rubber seals or stainless steel. The best on the market is, without doubt, the Danish-designed ProVino wine stopper with its three rubber O-rings, which create an airtight seal and even keep bubbles bubbling for days. ProVino stoppers are available from Sabato in Auckland, phone (09) 630 8751.
- DON'T keep wine in warm places. You might like it but the wine won't. Mulled wine is a different story, but we won't go there.
- DON'T store wine in the fridge unless you're planning to drink it soon. While the lack of oxygen in there will keep it fresh in the short term, the lack of humidity will dry out the cork in the long term, and that means one thing: oxidation.

- DON'T heat wine in the microwave for any more than 15–20 seconds (in a glass not a bottle, please!). Any more than this period of time will spoil the flavours of even the staunchest red. Believe me, I've worked long and hard experimenting with this!
- DON'T keep wine in the sun – light does destroy wine, except what's in your glass at the current time, of course.
- DON'T keep wine for too long. Every dog has its day, and most wines are made for immediate to medium-term consumption. If you're interested in aging wine, seek advice from the experts before making the investment.
- DO experiment with wines by opening them one day and enjoying a glass or two and then resealing them to see what flavours develop and open up over the next day.

WINE CELLARS

Temperature fluctuations and light kill wine quicker than anything else, so the perfect wine cellar conditions are those which are constant. Wine likes to be kept cool in the dark, but it also enjoys a little dampness, and its preferred temperature for long-term cellaring is 10–14 degrees Celsius. Most of us can only dream of giving our favourite wines these conditions, but what we can do is to emulate them as closely as possible. Choose a dark cupboard or place in the house that is not subject to heat or light fluctuations. Spare wardrobes, space under the stairs, or an unused linen cupboard are perfect places, so long as they are nowhere near to the hot-water cylinder!

The perfect cellar could be yours, for a price, but even if you do purchase a top-quality wine storage unit, it needs to be stored in such a way that light does not shine directly into it (unless you opt for one with an opaque door, of course).

Professional wine storage 'fridges' sell via **Wine Direct** in Auckland (no, this is not an advertisement) and take up about the same space as a large refrigerator, phone (09) 529 5267.

The Fine Wine Delivery Company rents out temperature- and humidity-controlled cellars in different sizes at a highly secure site in central Auckland, phone (09) 377 2300.

SERVING TEMPERATURES

If you like wine cool, just remember to chill it rather than kill it. Unlike light-flavoured beer, wine is not better served ice cold, but rather it loses most of its flavour and texture. Neither should you get bogged down with a thermometer stuck in the neck of your bottle just before you serve it. Instead, follow these few simple guidelines:

- Bubblies should be served chilled. Cool the bottle down in the fridge and serve it an ice bucket. Any bucket or container will do, just fill it with ice and a little water.
- Aromatic whites like müller-thurgau, gewürztraminer, riesling and sauvignon blanc do taste better with the warm edge taken off them a little. Twenty minutes in the average fridge will do nicely.
- Ditto dessert wines and stickies, which taste far better when they are cooled down, because this takes off their sweet edge without sacrificing flavour or that delicious, unctuous mouthfeel of really good dessert wines. Just remember, chilling does NOT mean ice cold!
- Most other whites taste just right served either at room temperature but if your rooms are in a warm, humid or hot climate, a few minutes in the fridge is probably highly desirable.
- Rosés and light reds like Beaujolais benefit from 10–20 minutes in the fridge. This accentuates their crisp and refreshing qualities.

- Most other reds are best served at room temperature, year-round. If it's really cold, a few seconds in the microwave will help (not the whole bottle!). Generally, no longer than 15–20 seconds per glass. And DON'T chill big, robust reds, it just makes them taste bitter and overtly tannic.
- Most importantly, do what feels good for you and be experimental.

BREIDECKER

Breidecker is a crossing of the müller-thurgau grape with the white grape hybrid, seibel. At best this grape makes refreshing, light whites with slightly floral aromas and a young life. The wines are best enjoyed young and do not have the potential to age.

★★★
$13-14

2002 Hunter's Breidecker Canterbury
Serve this light white wine chilled to bypass those slightly cloying sweet flavours, which are balanced by medium acids to give a crisp, refreshing flavour when cool.

 Hunter's Wines, Marlborough, phone (03) 572 8489, email: wine@hunters.co.nz or www.hunters.co.nz

CHARDONNAY

Chardonnay is the biggest selling wine and most planted grape variety in New Zealand, so it is no surprise to find that there are more wines in this chapter than in any other. And with over 130 to choose from, it was no mean feat picking a winner. This year the stand-out chardonnay is the 2002 Matua Matheson, which gets a whopping four out of five stars and has an attractively low price tag of just $18–19. This distinctive wine is made by Auckland-based winemaker Mark Robertson with grapes grown in Hawke's Bay. For years his wines have been winning medals, accolades and positive comments praising big body and subtlety – usually for higher-priced, more so-called serious wines than this little stunner.

Chardonnay now makes up 39 percent of this country's total vineyard area, mainly in Gisborne, Hawke's Bay and Marlborough but in tiny quantities everywhere else from Auckland to Central Otago. However, it is not just local wines that fill this chapter. Some of the best-value-for-money chardonnays available in this country flood in each year from Australia and increasingly also from Argentina, Chile and most excitingly from France – the spiritual home of this versatile grape variety.

★★★ 2001 Ashwood Grove Chardonnay
$15-16 Big and full-bodied with zing and freshness.

🛒 *Fine Wine Delivery Company and Village Winery, Auckland; The Mill Liquorsave; or contact Burleigh Trading for more stockists, phone (09) 480 0789.*

★★½ 2000 Astica Chardonnay
$11-12 Simple light chardonnay and just average value for money with its light lemony flavours and basic quaffing style.

🛒 *Beachaven Liquor, Auckland; Goldiggers, Thames; Pak 'N Save supermarkets, South Island; or contact Burleigh Trading for more stockists, phone (09) 480 0789.*

★★½ 2001 Babich East Coast Chardonnay
$15-16 Fresh, clean New Zealand chardonnay made with grapes grown on the east coast of the North Island. This tastes creamy and lightly fruity. It has a medium length.

🛒 *Widely available.*

★★½ 2002 Banrock Station Chardonnay
$14-15 Easy to enjoy summer white wine from Australia's Banrock Station, where the environment is treasured as much as the winemaking by the owners at parent-company BRL Hardy, which puts back a little money made from each bottle of this wine into saving endangered wetlands around the world. This is a light, basic chardonnay with a slightly drying finish but still good value.

🛒 *Widely available.*

★★★ 2001 Beresford Highwood Chardonnay
$15-16

A very light but refreshing clean, melon-tasting Australian chardonnay made from grapes grown in Padthaway, South Australia.

🛒 *Specialist wine stores nationwide, or for more detail contact Lace Wines, phone (09) 828 4725.*

★★ 2001 Beresford St Yvette Chardonnay
$14-15

An overtly creamy, buttery-tasting chardonnay with an over-the-top style. Average.

🛒 *Specialist wine stores nationwide, or for more detail contact Lace Wines, phone (09) 828 4725.*

★★★ 2002 Brajkovich Chardonnay
$18-19

Fresh off the bottling line three hours before tasting but still zingy, impressive and recognisably chardonnay in a subtle style. Michael Brajkovich reckons screwcaps give less bottle sickness immediately post-bottling, which accounts for why this wine tasted slightly spritzy in the mouth but still clean, fresh and lemony fruity. This is the first time this wine has not been made with 100 percent malolactic fermentation (the conversion of malic acids in grapes to softer lactic ones) and the wine benefits with a slightly austere but highly appealing flavour.

🛒 *Specialist wine stores, or at Kumeu River Wines, phone (09) 412 8415, email: enquiries@kumeuriver.co.nz, www.kumeuriver.co.nz*

★★★ 2002 Cairnbrae Marlborough Unoaked Chardonnay
$18-19

This refreshingly unoaked chardonnay is cool, crisp and defined by fruit flavour rather than oak or other creamy, buttery tastes that so often characterise chardonnays from this part of the planet. It is medium-bodied, fresh and lemon-tasting. Good value.

Specialist wine stores, or contact Cairnbrae Vineyards, phone (03) 572 8018, email: info@cairnbrae.co.nz

★★ 2001 Cheviot Bridge Chardonnay
$14-15

Pretty basic white chardonnay, full of oaky simple flavours and made in a relatively sweetish style.

Specialist wine stores.

★★½ 2001 Clifford Bay Marlborough Chardonnay
$18-19

Creamy big malo influence and very young when tasted. It seems a little oaky, over-the-top in style and a bit hot at the finish.

Most supermarkets and specialist wine stores.

★★½ 2000 Cockfighter's Ghost Hunter Valley Chardonnay
$18-19

Creamier version of the plain Jane below. Little fruit flavour is masked by the oak and leesy-malo taste, but this wine will have more appeal than its unoaked version.

Specialist wine stores, or from Macvine, phone (03) 570 2118.

★★ 2001 Cockfighter's Ghost Hunter Valley Unoaked Chardonnay
$18-19

A slightly plain chardonnay with hints of citrus flavour but a light body and short finish.

🛒 *Specialist wine stores, or from Macvine, phone (03) 570 2118.*

★★★ 2002 Collards Blakes Mill Chardonnay
$12-14

Simple fresh, pure fruity chardonnay with citrus flavours and fresh, lingering finish. Medium-bodied, great-value white wine.

🛒 *Widely available, or from Collards winery, phone (09) 838 8341.*

★★★★ 2002 Collards Hawke's Bay Chardonnay
$18-20

This seductively good chardonnay is further vindication, if any is needed, that Hawke's Bay is New Zealand's spiritual home of great chardonnay. I really love its varietal purity; it just tastes like unadulterated chardonnay with citrus freshness and lovely texture running through the palate. This is beautifully integrated, good value, fresh white wine.

🛒 *Widely available, or from Collards winery, phone (09) 838 8341.*

★★★ 2001 Cookoothama Darlington Point Chardonnay
$16-17

This is a creamy nuanced chardonnay with fresh, lingering flavours of lemon at the clean and crisp finish. Chardonnay-lovers will find it a reassuringly safe bet, especially at this price. Very good value for money.

🛒 *Specialist wine stores.*

★★★ $15-16
2002 Coopers Creek Gisborne Unoaked Chardonnay
It's a curious fact that so many New Zealand chardonnays taste sweet when in fact they are not very sweet at all, but the strident fruit flavour of grapes grown in places like Gisborne gives this wine an upfront fruitiness that redefines chardonnay as it has been known traditionally. Drink this one slightly chilled in the sunshine on a hot day with creamy cheese.
Foodtown, most wine stores.

★½ $13-14
2002 Corbans Chardonnay
Little character or fruit flavour in this very light, plain white.
Widely available.

★★★ $8-9
2002 Corbans White Label Chardonnay
Light yellow in colour, a fresh young wine with big acids on the front palate and overt malo-leesy characters, but not much going on in the sweet, ripe fruit spectrum. Still, very crisp and clean; it gets lots of points for that.
Widely available.

★★★ $9-10
2002 Cottlers Bridge Chardonnay
Soft and slightly creamy-textured, sweet-tasting but not cloying chardonnay. An easy-to-like, unchallenging, great-value-for-money drink.
Cellar Select and Wine Masters, Auckland; Advintage, Hastings. For South Island sales, contact Wine Masters, phone (09) 636 5240.

★★★ 2001 Culemborg Chardonnay
$10-11

This is fantastic value for money with lovely smooth creamy flavours that add body to this light-to-medium-bodied wine without overwhelming its light citrusy tastes. Very good value for money at this price.

🍷 *Liquor stores and supermarkets, or contact Federal Geo for stockists, phone (09) 578 1823, email: federalgeo@xtra.co.nz*

★★½ 1999 d'Arenberg The Olive Grove Chardonnay
$15-17

The grapes were grown in McLaren Vale for this wine, which is very Australian, very ripe, sweet fruity but a little over-the-top, perhaps. Not brilliant but clean and has a lovely smooth, creamy texture.

🍷 *Specialist wine stores.*

★★½ 2002 Deakin Estate Chardonnay
$12-13

Here is a highly polished, low-priced, great-value-for-money chardonnay. It doesn't have all the bells and whistles some chardonnay-lovers might expect, but it is an honest, clean little white for barbecues and parties.

🍷 *Widely available.*

★★ 2000 Deen De Bortoli Vat 7 Chardonnay
$14-15

Think of cream and spice and you have this one-dimensional white summed up. It's very big in flavour, oozing buttery tastes for those who like their chardonnays that way. Average value for money, since the fruit flavours barely shine through.

🍷 *Widely available.*

★★★ 2000 Delegat's Hawke's Bay Chardonnay
$14-15

Big buttery aromas lead into a creamy style of chardonnay made with grapes grown in Hawke's Bay and just a tad over-the-top in style, with all those creamy nuances in front of fruit flavour. If you like your chardonnay big and bold, you will love this wine, and it is good value for money.

♛ *Liquor King stores, Countdown, Foodtown, New World, Pak 'N Save, Woolworths.*

★★★½ 2002 Delegat's Reserve Chardonnay
$19-20

There are plenty of reasons to opt with your wallet and your tastebuds and buy this big, rich-flavoured chardonnay. Its cedary aromas and spicy flavours are kept in a tight muscly body, and this wine also oozes ripe flavours of nectarines and apricots.

♛ *Liquor King, Countdown, Foodtown, New World, Pak 'N Save, Woolworths.*

★★★ 2001 Domaine Corsin Saint-Veran
$19-20

This French chardonnay will instantly win fans with its rounded, fruity, caramel flavours and long finish. Very good value. If you can't find it at your nearest specialist wine store, you can get it by mail order.

♛ *Specialist wine stores, or contact Wine Direct for a store near you, or for mail order, freephone 0800 660 777.*

★★★½ **2001 Domaine Sainte Claire Petit Chablis**
$19-20
It's wines like this fresh-tasting French chardonnay that make wine-lovers flock to the doors of Paul Mitchell's Wine Direct warehouse, tucked away in an obscure street in Newmarket, Auckland. This lemony chablis is true to style, crisp and with a medium finish. It is not only good value for money but also an excellent introduction to classic chablis that tastes like wine rather than like the buttery or oaky flavours so often found in chardonnay.

🛒 *Specialist wine stores, or contact Wine Direct for a store near you, or for mail order, freephone 0800 660 777.*

★★★ **2002 Drylands Marlborough Chardonnay**
$18-19
Stylish chardonnay made from grapes grown in Marlborough where the climate imbues wines like this with a fresh, zingy acid finish, adding to its overall balance and length. This is a creamy-tasting wine but with fresh nectarine flavours in the mix too. Good value.

🛒 *Widely available.*

★★★ **2001 Duca di Castelmonte Centare Inzolia Chardonnay**
$18-19
Chardonnay-lovers will enjoy this wine hugely, although technically this Italian white belongs in the chapter relating to other white wines, since it is a blend of inzolia and chardonnay grapes. It tastes deliciously rounded and flavoursome, with hints of grapefruit and lemon held in check in a medium-acid, medium-bodied style. Great value at this price and very food-friendly.

🛒 *Specialist wine stores, or contact importer Phil Clark at A Touch of Italy, phone (09) 273 3701, email: sales@touchofitaly.co.nz*

★★ 2002 Eaglehawk Chardonnay
$12-13

Sweet, coconutty aromas hit the tastebuds when you sip this Australian chardonnay, which seems to be more about the oak than the fruit flavours. It is a little drying on the finish and really only offers basic drinking.

🛒 *Widely available.*

★★½ 2002 Equinox Hawke's Bay Chardonnay
$19-20

Ripe, rounded Hawke's Bay chardonnay with fresh but light flavours of nectarines and fleshy peaches. A very good everyday quaffing white with body to burn and a good price tag.

🛒 *Equinox Wines, email: sales@equinoxwines.co.nz*

★★★½ 2002 Esk Valley Hawke's Bay Chardonnay
$19-20

Fresh, bright, nicely rounded chardonnay in a crisp, typically Chablis-like style.

🛒 *Widely available.*

★★ 2002 Fat Cat Chardonnay
$14-15

Fantastic label of a cat lying back vulgarly with a cigar, but a pretty overblown creamy, sweet Kiwi chardonnay made with grapes grown in Gisborne, where they often taste like this. It is a hefty 14 percent alcohol, so if that over-the-top flavour doesn't get you, the alcohol will.

🛒 *Foodtown, New World, Pak 'N Save, Woolworths.*

★★½ 2002 Fernleaf Chardonnay
$10-11

This is a lively chardonnay with a very light body but loads of appealing zesty lemon flavours and nicely balanced acids stretching out the wine to a medium finish. Good value entry-level chardonnay in a very appealing style.

🛒 *Widely available.*

★★ **2001 Firestick Mount Compass Langhorne Creek Chardonnay**
$18-19

This is a bit of a plain Jane Aussie chardonnay with little to commend it beyond the realms of basic everyday drinking. It's clean and plain and a little pricey.

🧺 Specialist wine stores, or from Macvine, phone (03) 570 2118.

★★½ **2001 Giesen Marlborough Chardonnay**
$16-17

Fresh, young but slightly green-tasting chardonnay made with grapes grown in Marlborough. This is pretty average value for money.

🧺 Foodtown, Woolworths, or contact Burleigh Trading for more stockists, phone (09) 480 0789.

★★★ **2001 Goldridge Estate Hawke's Bay Chardonnay**
$15-16

Lovely rounded fruity chardonnay with lots of attractive spicy oaky flavours, which are far more integrated into this wine style than the winery's Marlborough chardonnay, below. Great value at this price and a style that will find loads of fans.

🧺 Foodtown, specialist wine stores and liquor retailers.

★★½ **2001 Goldridge Estate Marlborough Chardonnay**
$18-19

It's no surprise to find that this wine has been fermented in oak, because there is a hefty aroma of wood in each whiff of this slightly austere little number. It's rewardingly medium-to-full-bodied but average value at this price.

🧺 Foodtown, specialist wine stores and liquor retailers.

★★★½ **2001 Gramps Chardonnay**
$15-16 I like this big, bold, oaky-tasting Australian chardonnay. And at this price it has it all: drinkability, affordability and, most importantly, lots of well-balanced, lingering flavours of citrus and clean freshness.
Specialist wine stores.

★★½ **2002 Gunn Estate Unoaked Chardonnay**
$14-15 Gunn Estate winery takes its name from owner Denis Gunn and is situated in the Ohiti Valley in sunny Hawke's Bay. This is a lightly creamy, fresh chardonnay with tropical flavours of melon, pineapple and grapefruit.
Specialist wine stores.

★★★ **2001 Hanging Rock Winery Chardonnay**
$15-16 The minimalist packaging is a foil for the flavoursome funky chardonnay inside this bottle – funky not because it's typical chardonnay but rather because of its restrained, clean focus on flavours of light spice and citrus. Lovely balance. Great price.
Glengarry, North Island; other specialist wine stores nationwide.

★★½ **Hardys Chardonnay**
$8-9 Lightly fruity chardonnay with creamy smooth texture and medium finish. Good value for everyday drinking white.
Widely available.

★★½ 2002 Hardys Varietal Range Chardonnay
$9-10 This South Australian chardonnay has crisp lemon flavours and a vigorous, slightly aggressive acid structure, which seems to cut the wine short just a tad at the finish. Still, at this price it is good value for basic drinking white.
🛒 *Widely available.*

★★★ 1999 Henry Lawson Chardonnay
$16-17 A crisp, lemon-tasting Australian chardonnay that is good value for money and refreshingly honest in style with fruit flavour and zing leading the way in each mouthful.
🛒 *Specialist wine stores.*

★★½ 2002 Houghton Chardonnay
$12-13 West Australian chardonnay with slightly citrus flavours and an off-dry finish. Average stuff but good spending if you want a clean, simple barbecue white.
🛒 *Widely available.*

★★ 2000 Huntaway Reserve Gisborne Chardonnay
$19-20 Even a second bottle of this wine failed to reveal anything much to commend – it was green and grassy-tasting and still relatively dirty in flavour. The first was oxidised flat fruit flavours and the cork came out pretty easily. There's nothing left here but sourness.
🛒 *Liquor stores and specialist wine stores.*

★★★ Jackman Ridge Chardonnay
$8-9 Fresh and clean and although quite sweet this is an honest wine with purity of flavour and nothing else cluttering it up. Very good value for money.
🛒 *Widely available.*

★★★½ 2001 Jacob's Creek Reserve Chardonnay
$19-20

Great value wine, this Australian big-brand chardonnay. It might be mass-produced, but it has lovely balance of flavour erring in the clean, grapefruity and lemon direction. Fantastically drinkable.

Widely available.

★★½ 2001 Jamiesons Run Limestone Coast Chardonnay
$14-15

A relatively cool-climate wine with slight green tendencies aromatically and also with a slightly drying, astringent-type finish. A bit disappointing.

Widely available.

★★★ 2002 Kemblefield Winemakers Signature Chardonnay
$16-17

This Hawke's Bay wine has zingy fresh acids and a surprisingly clean, fresh style. I like its purity of flavour, with a hint of stonefruit nectarine and flashes of pineapple, but essentially this is pure, unadulterated chardonnay allowed to shine. And a great price too!

Point Wines and Cellar Select, Auckland; The Merchant of Taupo; Advintage, Hastings; Invercargill Licensing Trust; or from the winery, phone (06) 874 9649, email: kew@kemblefield.co.nz

★★★½ 2002 Kim Crawford Unoaked Marlborough Chardonnay
$19-20

Lovely zingy pure and fresh chardonnay that is refreshing unfettered by oaky nuances. I love this wine. It is chardonnay as it should be and it tastes ripe, fresh, tropical and lingering.

Glengarry, North Island; specialist wine stores nationwide.

★★½ 2001 Kingston Chardonnay
$15-16
This fresh little Australian white is creamy and spicy but tastes a little too overtly woody. At this price it represents average value for money.

The Mill Liquorsave and some supermarkets, or contact Burleigh Trading for more stockists, phone (09) 480 0789.

★★½ 2001 Knappstein Clare Valley Chardonnay
$19-20
A creamy-tasting Australian chardonnay with a smooth texture and lingering, buttery finish. Highly appealing, though slightly one-dimensional.

Liquor King and specialist wine stores.

★★ 2000 KWV Chardonnay
$12-13
Very watery-tasting South African chardonnay with a slightly thin finish.

Liquor stores and supermarkets, or contact Federal Geo for stockists, phone (09) 578 1823, email: federalgeo@xtra.co.nz

★★½ 2002 Lake Chalice Marlborough Unoaked Chardonnay
$17-19
For an unoaked wine this could be fresher. It is medium- to full-bodied with stonefruity flavours of peaches and a creamy mid-palate but a little lean.

Glengarry and some other specialist wine stores, or Lake Chalice Wines, phone (03) 572 9327, email: wine@lakechalice.co.nz

★★½ 2002 Lake Chalice Marlborough Vineyard Selection Chardonnay
$18-20

Full-on creamy nuances dominate this wine's nose and palate, subduing the fruit a little. It does have a lovely dry finish but the barrel fermentation in this wine (40 percent), is relatively overt.

Where to buy: Glengarry and some other specialist wine stores, or Lake Chalice Wines, phone (03) 572 9327, email: wine@lakechalice.co.nz

★★½ 2002 Lincoln Winemakers Series Gisborne Chardonnay
$14-15

Lovely bright, fresh, clean chardonnay but tastes a little like its own cork although not tainted. Best drunk young and slightly chilled at a picnic with salty meat, when its freshness will be most enjoyed.

Liquorland and Cellar Select, or contact Lincoln Vineyards, phone (09) 838 6944, email: wine@lincolnwines.co.nz

★★★ 2002 Lindemans Bin 65 Chardonnay
$12-13

When wine scribes and judges call something elegant, it can be a little difficult to determine exactly what they mean, but one sip of this will probably help tell you. It's a subtle white with chardonnay's hallmark creamy nuances but well-balanced fruit and medium body to counter that. Great value at this price.

Widely available.

★★★ 2002 Lindemans Cawarra Chardonnay
$9-10

Clean, fresh and great value. This wine has sweet lemon flavours balanced with a lingering oaky finish. Okay, it's not hugely complex, but it has a pure chardonnay flavour, which is all too rare these days.

Widely available.

★★★ 2001 Lindemans Padthaway Chardonnay
$18-19

Big, bold Australian chardonnay, which is exactly what most drinkers want. It's a tad over-the-top in its caramelly creamy flavours, which mask the stonefruit lying underneath. For all that, this wine will find instant fans.

🛒 *Widely available.*

★★½ 2002 Longridge Hawke's Bay Chardonnay
$14-15

This good-value little beauty proves that, even at this entry level of quality, Hawke's Bay is home to the best chardonnay grapes in New Zealand, with warm, nectarine, fresh flavours like this. Medium-bodied and a pretty short finish but good value for a simple everyday, dryish white.

🛒 *Widely available.*

★★ 2001 Lucknow Estate Marlborough Chardonnay
$19-20

Very lean, green-tasting chardonnay made from grapes that do not taste fully ripe. Simple and a bit overpriced.

🛒 *New World in Lower Hutt and Wellington, and at Lucknow Estate, phone (06) 874 9007, email: lucknow@xtra.co.nz*

★★½ 2000 McPherson's Chardonnay
$13-14

The strident fruity flavours in this wine give it a sweetish taste that is probably more to do with Australia's hot climate than any actual sweetness in the wine. It's tropical, rounded, medium-bodied and good value if you like big, obvious, buttery-styled chardonnay.

🛒 *Liquor stores and supermarkets, or contact Federal Geo for stockists, phone (09) 578 1823, email: federalgeo@xtra.co.nz*

★★ **2000 Maglieri of McLaren Vale Chardonnay**
$16-18
This is a big, buttery-tasting chardonnay that is slightly losing its grip now, developing into a deeply yellow-hued wine that needs to be consumed soon. Okay value for money, or look for the next vintage, due out soon, which will be fresher and livelier.
🛒 *Widely available.*

★★½ **2001 Main Divide Chardonnay**
$18-19
The second label of Pegasus Bay Winery in Waipara, made with grapes grown in Canterbury and Marlborough. Has an instantly recognisable creamy chardonnay elegance but a slightly sour finish.
🛒 *Specialist wine stores, or Pegasus Bay Wines, phone (03) 314 6869.*

★★★ **2001 Manara Rock Limestone Coast Chardonnay**
$14-15
I like this fresh, clean chardonnay with its pure, fresh fruit flavours and spicy, almost aniseed freshness. A delicious, honest chardonnay offering far more pure flavours than most chardonnays, especially at this absolutely bargain price. Buy a case!
🛒 *Widely available.*

★★★ **2001 Matariki Stony Bay Chardonnay**
$18-19
Good, honest, very-good-value chardonnay made from grapes grown in Hawke's Bay. This wine tastes of fresh sweet lemons and grapefruit, and has a medium body and finish.
🛒 *The Mill Liquorsave; Main Street Cellars, Waiuku; Birds Liquorsave, Thames; Corporate Direct, Wellington; Matariki Winery, Hawke's Bay, or from the website: www.matarikiwines.co.nz*

Matthew Lang Chardonnay

★★ — $8-9

Very light, very woody in flavour and slightly drying on the finish. Not great value.

Widely available.

2002 Matua Eastern Bays Chardonnay

★★½ — $15-16

A relatively basic chardonnay made with grapes grown in various regions in New Zealand. Basic entry-level wine made in a clean, if ubiquitous, style.

Widely available.

2002 Matua Matheson Chardonnay

★★★★ — $18-19 — **STAR BUY**

For many wine-lovers it is this style of chardonnay that first made them fall in love with the world's most popular white wine. It is fresh, dry and flavoursome in a crisp fashion, bordering on citrusy-lemon in taste but not at all over-the-top. And it is a classically good Hawke's Bay dry white, an absolute steal at this price. Fantastic wine!

Widely available.

2002 Matua Valley Settler Chardonnay

★★½ — $11-12

Fresh, clean chardonnay with bright aromas and flavours of citrus fruit and a hint of stonefruit. Good value everyday-drinking white wine.

Widely available.

★★★ **2001 Michel Laroche Chardonnay**
$16-17
Fantastically good value French chardonnay from the South of France, which is, refreshingly, unhampered by the sometimes denigrating words 'vin de pays'. Yes, this wine is from the country, but it is far superior to most people's preconceptions about 'country wines'. Crisp, clean, lemony but not austere, this is a friendly, heart-warming wine that says 'drink me now'.
Specialist wine stores.

★★ **2001 Mills Reef Hawke's Bay Chardonnay**
$14-15
Mid-yellow colour with a creamy aroma and slightly interesting grainy texture but a bit sickly Kiwi chardonnay. Plain Jane with all the cheap bells and whistles of quaffable chardonnay.
Widely available in supermarkets and wine stores nationwide, or contact Mills Reef Winery, phone (07) 576 8800.

★★★½ **2001 Mills Reef Hawke's Bay Reserve Chardonnay**
$19-20
A big-bodied chardonnay with lovely round body and edges and flavours of ripe tropical nectarines. Very good value. It costs more but it delivers impressively.
Widely available in supermarkets and wine stores nationwide, or contact Mills Reef Winery, phone (07) 576 8800.

★★½ **2001 Millstream Chardonnay**
$10-11
Lightish chardonnay but good value at this rock-bottom price. It has body and texture that many wines a few dollars more lack. Great buying for everyday light drinking.
Liquor stores and supermarkets, or contact Federal Geo for stockists, phone (09) 578 1823, email: federalgeo@xtra.co.nz

★★ 2002 Mission Estate Hawke's Bay Chardonnay
$14-16

There is no equivalent English description for the French 'vin ordinaire', but like many chardonnays this one fits that bill. It is clean and creamy, as chardonnay-lovers like it but otherwise a bit of a plain Jane.

🍷 *Widely available, or from Mission Estate Winery, phone (06) 844 2259.*

★★★ 2002 Montana Gisborne Chardonnay
$14-15

Lovely wine. Light- to medium-yellow colour with an appealing tropical fruity nose and soft acids, well balanced against the fruit flavours. Finish is medium in length but more than acceptable, luring you via its clean, fruity spectrum to enjoy another sip or two. An easy-to-enjoy, fresh, medium-bodied white.

🍷 *Widely available.*

★★½ 2002 Murray Ridge Chardonnay
$9-10

Creamy, which makes you think 'chardonnay' immediately, but this is very light in body and gets a decent flavour from sweetness and a dollop of oak chips – at least it tastes that way. Not bad value for a sweetish low-end chardonnay for everyday drinking.

🍷 *Widely available.*

★★★ 2002 Ngatarawa Stables Chardonnay
$15-16

Chardonnay flows in the veins of the Corban family, including Ngatarawa winemaker Alwyn Corban, who demonstrates this with a lively, fresh young wine that positively oozes lemon citrus style in a restrained, subtle style. This is deliciously drinkable and brilliantly priced.

🍷 *Restaurants and at the Ngatarawa Wines Cellar Door, Hawke's Bay, phone (06) 879 7603, email: ngatarawawines@clear.net.nz*

★★ **2002 Nobilo Fall Harvest Chardonnay**
$14-15 Very light, plain chardonnay with a hint of buttery taste in the mid-palate but a short finish.
🧺 *Widely available.*

★★★ **2001 Nobilo Poverty Bay Chardonnay**
$14-15 Here's a chardonnay for those who like them big and obvious with full-on flavours of malolactic-derived creaminess in both taste and texture. This wine is soft and medium-bodied. Good value.
🧺 *Widely available.*

★★ **Nobilo White Cloud Chardonnay**
$8-9 Light, fresh, relatively basic chardonnay with an overt creamy taste and not much else – bar an enticing price tag.
🧺 *Widely available.*

★½ **2002 Nottage Hill Chardonnay**
$11-12 Lean, acidic Australian chardonnay with little warmth or fruit flavour. Very basic white.
🧺 *Widely available.*

★★★ **2001 Odyssey Reserve Chardonnay**
$18-20 Auckland winemaker Rebecca Salmond makes this wine from grapes grown on the Kawitiri Vineyard in Gisborne. It has had eight months contact with its lees (dead yeast cells) which imbue the wine with a lovely savoury, textural quality and flavour. Great-value chardonnay in a full-bodied, big Gisborne style.
🧺 *Specialist wine stores, or contact Odyssey Wines, phone (09) 837 5410, odyssey.wines@xtra.co.nz*

★★★ $19-20 2001 Okahu Estate Shipwreck Bay Northland Chardonnay

Fresh, lively, citrusy chardonnay with gorgeously refreshing qualities and soft, ripe sweet fruit flavours and textures. None of the malo thing over-the-top here at all. Just gorgeous ripe fruit.

Specialist wine stores, or Okahu Estate, phone (09) 408 0888.

★★½ $13-14 2001 Old Coach Road Chardonnay

This chardonnay encapsulates all that many love and some loathe about chardonnay. This is a big, creamy creature that is fresh and nicely balanced with vibrant acids in a medium-bodied style, but the fruit is a little lost in all the creaminess.

Widely available.

★★★ $19-20 2000 Orlando St Hillary Chardonnay

A classic Australian chardonnay with oodles of oak, buttery flavours and a slightly zingy finish that adds finesse to its otherwise full-on style. This wine will find fans everywhere. Great value for money at this price.

Specialist wine stores.

★★ $18-20 2001 Pencarrow Martinborough Chardonnay

Sickly creamy malo and leesy character in the mouth but clean and fresh with perhaps a little less than fully ripe grapes used adding acid but not much else.

Specialist wine stores, or Palliser Estate Wines, phone (06) 306 9019, email: Palliser@palliser.co.nz or www.palliser.co.nz

★★★½
$17-18

2001 Penfolds Koonunga Hill Chardonnay
Great stuff! Not least because those luscious fruity flavours actually linger at the finish, which lasts long after you have had your last sip. This is very-good-value chardonnay, full of flavoursome nectarine and stonefruit tastes and with a creamy texture to it. Buy at least half a case.
🛒 *Widely available.*

★★½
$13-14

2002 Penfolds Rawson's Retreat Chardonnay
Tasted at the Hilton, Auckland, led by the fourth-ever chief winemaker at Penfolds, Peter Gago. Very fresh peachy-flavoured chardonnay with crisp but soft acids, nicely balanced, medium-length finish. Very good value for money although has a bit of a hole mid-palate, but it has a fresh, clean style.
🛒 *Widely available.*

★★★
$17-18

2001 Preece Chardonnay
This tall, stylish bottle contains an elegant-tasting, crisp chardonnay with vibrant flavours of lemon and pineapple, and lingering length. Good value for money.
🛒 *Liquor King and specialist wine stores.*

★★
$9-10

2002 Queen Adelaide Chardonnay
This is my least favourite white in the well-known Queen Adelaide stable of wines. Often good but this year just a little bit too obvious and overblown in flavour. However, it tastes like chardonnay from the first whiff – if you associate chardonnay with oak and cream, that is. Average value for money, even with an all-time low price.
🛒 *Widely available.*

CHARDONNAY

★★½ **2001 Redbank Long Paddock Chardonnay**
$14-15 Clean, fresh and simple. I like the pure fruity flavours here, although they are light.
🍷 *Specialist wine stores.*

★★★ **Richmond Grove Padthaway Chardonnay**
$18-19 Lovely rounded, creamy-textured Australian chardonnay with a medium-to-big body and a very-good-value price tag.
🍷 *Widely available.*

★★ **2002 Riverside Wines Chardonnay**
$14-16 This is a very fresh but slightly green-tasting chardonnay made from grapes grown inland from the city of Napier in Hawke's Bay. It's a little acidic in style and is best suited to have with food rather than on its own. Drink it with fishcakes or fresh fish.
🍷 *Big Fresh, Foodtown, Woolworths, or from Riverside Wines, phone (06) 844 4942, email: riverside.wines@xtra.co.nz*

★★½ **2002 Robard & Butler Chardonnay**
$10-11 Light and fresh with hints of citrusy sharpness to add tang to its soft texture. Good value for money for basic drinking but nothing special for the tastebuds.
🍷 *Widely available.*

★★ **2001 Roberts Rock Chenin Chardonnay**
$12-13 Light white blend of chenin blanc and chardonnay grapes. The crisp acids balance the creamy nuance but otherwise this wine is a little light and short.
🍷 *Liquor stores and supermarkets, or contact Federal Geo for stockists, phone (09) 578 1823, email: federalgeo@xtra.co.nz*

★★★ **2002 Rosemount Estate Chardonnay**
$15-16
This Australian chardonnay is clean and fresh with a medium-sweet, fruity finish that even lingers a little. The style is light but this is good value for a pure chardonnay taste.
🛒 *Widely available.*

★★ **Ruben Hall Chardonnay**
$9-10
A slightly green-tasting, easily affordable chardonnay that is thin on the finish and short. Pretty basic quaffing wine.
🛒 *Widely available.*

★★★ **2001 Sacred Hill Barrel Fermented Hawke's Bay Chardonnay**
$19-20
Very keenly priced wine with nice textural qualities gained from the malolactic fermentation, which adds something but also subtracts on the palate from the fruit flavour by dominating it with creamy flavours and aromas. It's a tad simplistic and one-dimensional but lovely texturally. Guess it'll gain fans on both points.
🛒 *Widely available.*

★★½ **2002 Sacred Hill Whitecliff Estate Unoaked Chardonnay**
$14-15
Creamy and clean but stylistically not that creative, just the same old chardonnay thing well made from Hawke's Bay grapes. Move up a notch (above) to find the real story.
🛒 *Widely available.*

★★★ 2002 Saint Clair Marlborough Chardonnay
$19-20

Smooth, savoury-tasting, creamy and a big step up from the unoaked Saint Clair chardonnay (below). It is a little grippy at the finish but very tasty with savoury nibble food or just on its own at the end of the day.

Widely available.

★★½ 2002 Saint Clair Marlborough Unoaked Chardonnay
$16-17

Fresh, simple white, suitable for everyday quaffing, and since it is unfettered by oak it is a light wine that is especially easy to enjoy in the middle of the day.

Widely available.

★★½ 2001 St Hallett Poachers Chardonnay
$16-17

Very likeable but slightly over-the-top Australian chardonnay, but I do like its robust textural finish. Great quality for the price with its grainy, savoury flavours and long, lingering finish. Tasty.

Glengarry, Liquor King, Liquorland, specialist wine stores.

★★★ 2002 Saints Chardonnay
$16-17

Clean, crisp, pure chardonnay made from grapes grown in Gisborne by New Zealand's largest wine company, Montana Wines. This is very good value for money at well below $20 for what is a relatively subtle style from one of the country's most northern chardonnay-producing regions.

Widely available.

★★★ 2002 Saints Gisborne Chardonnay
$16-17

Like most chardonnays made from Gisborne grapes, this is big and creamy in texture and has massive appeal. Its strident fruit flavours taste sweet but not cloying, and it has a lingering soft finish. This is very good value.

Widely available.

★★ 2002 Sanctuary Marlborough Chardonnay
$14-15

A basic chardonnay with overtly sweet flavours in an over-the-top malo-styled wine.

Most supermarkets and some specialist wine stores.

★★½ 2001 Sandalford Element Chardonnay
$15-16

Light, lemony-tasting chardonnay with high acids, demanding some simple food to soften down the wine. Drink it with fish.

The Mill Liquorsave or contact Burleigh Trading for more stockists, phone (09) 480 0789.

★★ 2001 Seifried Estate Chardonnay
$19-20

Much better than the Old Coach Road, this is fresh and vibrant chardonnay with shiny clean nectarine flavours and a hint of lemonade flavour. Medium length, reasonable value and tasty wine.

Widely available.

★★½ 2002 Selaks Marlborough Chardonnay
$14-15

Rich, creamy style of chardonnay from Marlborough with all the bells and whistles that chardonnay-lovers long for. It has a medium body but lingering flavoursome finish with spicy flavours intermingling with a buttery taste.

Widely available.

★★½ 2002 Shingle Peak Marlborough Chardonnay
$19-20
This light white made from grapes grown in Marlborough is fresh and clean but just a tad austere in texture. Average value.

🛒 *Widely available.*

★★ 2002 Silky Oak Chardonnay
$12-13
Fresh and clean but a little green-tasting on the finish, which is a tad grippy.

🛒 *Liquor stores and supermarkets, or contact Federal Geo for stockists, phone (09) 578 1823, email: federalgeo@xtra.co.nz*

★★½ 2001 Sir James Chardonnay
$17-18
Toasty, spicy, citrusy-lemon-tasting chardonnay from Australia. This wine has a lightly grippy finish, but it is good value for money for those who like their chardonnays big, bold and obvious in style.

🛒 *Liquorland stores.*

★★★ 2001 Spy Valley Marlborough Chardonnay
$19-20
Clean, fresh, flavoursome chardonnay with a hint of creaminess that ends, refreshingly, mid-palate. Made by North Canterbury-based winemaker Alan McCorkindale from three different clones of chardonnay. It is just off-dry in style, which suits the style of the grapes. Good value for elegant wine drinking.

🛒 *Liquorland stores; Moore Wilson, Wellington; specialist wine stores; or contact the winery for more stockists, phone (03) 572 9840, email: j.estate@xtra.co.nz*

★★★   2001 Stoneleigh Chardonnay
$17-18

Good quality, well-made wine but relies heavily on creamy malolactic influence to soften out the sharp, harsh acids of Marlborough fruit. I like the fruit, which is possibly a little lean without that softening malo effect, but this is still good value.

🧺 *Widely available.*

★★½   2001 Stony Bay Chardonnay
$19-20

A bit of a plain Jane with little to distinguish it from the whole wide world full of chardonnays except for a relatively lingering finish and a crisp, green, New Zealand taste – like biting into a fresh Granny Smith. Good wine for chardonnay-lovers to drink during a hot sunny day when it will taste refreshing and clean.

🧺 *Specialist wine stores and at Matariki Wines, phone (06) 879 6226, email: wine@matarikiwines.co.nz*

★★★½   2001 Tasman Bay Marlborough Chardonnay
$18-19

This stunningly textural, full-bodied and subtle chardonnay is one of the jewels in the crown of the Nelson wine label Tasman Bay. Winemakers Phil Jones and Matthew Rutherford have styled an incredibly elegant, flavoursome and lingering-tasting chardonnay, which has flavours of fresh apples, a hint of lemon and a creamy, rounded finish. Brilliant value for money.

🧺 *Widely available.*

★★★   2001 Tatachilla Partners Chardonnay
$17-18

Lovely fresh acids and creamy nuances and a plain, chardonnay-like finish. Grapey and clean and fresh. Lovely and new tasting.

🧺 *Foodtown, New World, Woolworths, specialist wine stores.*

★★★ 2002 Taylors Clare Valley Chardonnay
$16-17
Clean, fruity Australian chardonnay with lovely fresh flavours that nod in the grapefruit, red apple and lemon direction. Good value.
Widely available.

★★½ 2001 Taylors Estate Chardonnay
$14-15
This is a more predictable style of chardonnay than its unwooded stablemate. Big, bold and creamy and pretty spicy from oak on the palate.
Widely available.

★★★½ 2001 Taylors Promised Land Unwooded Chardonnay
$14-15
This is a fabulous creamy-textured wine that actually tastes of chardonnay. Ripe, sweet, fresh citrus flavours – think ripe fresh lemons and grapefruit and you've hit the nail on the head. Fantastic stuff.
Widely available.

★★★ 2002 Te Awa Farm Longlands Chardonnay
$19-20
This Hawke's Bay winery changed hands late last year, so let's hope its wines continue their reputation for quality. This is a fresh, bright young white, which is what good-quality chardonnay is all about: zingy, medium-bodied and flavoursome while also showing a lovely balance of body, flavour and texture.
Widely available.

★★ 2002 Timara Oak Aged Chardonnay
$9-10
It's hard to believe this earthy-textured little white has been aged in oak, although it does taste woody in a drying type of way.
Widely available.

★★★ 1999 Trapiche Oak Cask Chardonnay
$18-19

This Argentinian chardonnay is great value for money. Fresh, flavoursome and deliciously full-bodied, it has butterscotch flavours with rounded spiciness coming from the oak in the wine.

📛 *Wine Masters, Auckland; Regional Wines, Wellington; Cellar Select; or contact Burleigh Trading for more stockists, phone (09) 480 0789.*

★★½ 2001 Trinity Hill Shepherds Croft Hawke's Bay Chardonnay
$18-19

Fresh, creamy chardonnay which is a second label from John Hancock, the man once renowned for making great chardonnays but now more focused on reds. This is a delicious creamy, textural wine, spicy with a medium-length finish.

📛 *Widely available, or contact the winery, phone (09) 879 7778, www.trinityhillwines.com*

★★★ 2001 Twin Islands Chardonnay
$15-16

Light, fresh, creamy and smooth. Offers above-average value for money in a clean, fresh style with good length, although not a lot of character.

📛 *Big Fresh, Woolworths, specialist wine stores.*

★★½ 2001 Tyrrell's Long Flat Vineyard Chardonnay
$12-13

Affordable everyday white for when you just want a drink rather than something special. This wine tastes a little dusty around the edges but provides reasonable value for a simple white.

📛 *Widely available.*

★★★ 2001 Tyrrell's Old Winery Chardonnay
$15-16
This is a lovely textural wine with creamy flavours supported by hefty, some would say too much, oak that adds savoury spice to the taste of the wine. It's big, bold and unashamedly Australian in style but offers pleasure to those ever-present chardonnay-lovers.
Widely available.

★★½ 2002 Tyrrell's Wines Moore's Creek Chardonnay
$13-14
A light chardonnay that is reliably clean and fresh but fairly one-dimensional in taste. Average value for money.
Glengarry, North Island.

★★★½ 2002 Vidal Estate Hawke's Bay Chardonnay
$17-18
Sealed with a screwcap, this is a zingy fresh chardonnay and is the perfect thing to drink with roast chicken or even on its own in the sun. It is bottled sunshine, clean and tasty with creamy textures.
Widely available.

★★ 2002 Villa Maria Cellar Selection Marlborough Chardonnay
$19-20
A slightly creamy-nuanced chardonnay with a staunch acid bite to its finish.
Widely available.

★★★½ Villa Maria East Coast Vintage Selection Chardonnay Chenin Blanc
$10-11
Fantastically fresh blend of chardonnay and chenin blanc grapes to make this gorgeously bright, zingy, peachy-tasting wine. Has a dry finish and makes a fabulous food wine or is lovely on its own. Great value.
Widely available.

★★★ 2002 Villa Maria Private Bin Chardonnay
$15-16

Fresh, clean chardonnay with vibrant citrus aromas and fresh acid bite. A good everyday drinking chardonnay, which will be magic with fresh fish.

🧺 *Widely available.*

★★★½ 2002 Waimea Estate Chardonnay
$19-20

This chardonnay will win instant fans. And rightly so, since it is packed with flavours of fresh fruit, hinting at nectarines and grapefruit but so nicely balanced with vigorous acids and medium body that nothing sticks out above anything else. This is a great buy. Delicious and lingering and good value for money.

🧺 *Liquor King, Liquorland and most supermarkets.*

★★½ 2002 Wally's Hut Chardonnay
$11-12

This light-bodied Australian chardonnay is classically ocker in style from its over-the-top buttery aroma that leads into similar flavours. It has a relatively short finish, delivering average flavour and value for money.

🧺 *Glengarry, North Island; or phone (09) 379 3740.*

★★½ 2002 Wolf Blass Chardonnay
$14-15

Simple, light and fresh. Reasonable value for a basic everyday quaffing chardonnay.

🧺 *Widely available.*

★★★ **2001 Wyndham Estate 1828 Unwooded Chardonnay**
$9-10
Simple, light Australian chardonnay that is uncluttered by oak or other winemaker tricks but also relatively basic. Still, it is dry in style and, although it is slightly short at the finish, I would choose this over two-thirds of the other chardonnays here, simply for its pure, honest flavours. Very good value.
🧺 *Widely available.*

★★½ **2001 Wyndham Estate Bin 222 Chardonnay**
$12-13
A slightly plain Australian chardonnay with sweet oaky flavours buoyed up with a spicy taste. Its off-dry fruit style makes it easy to enjoy and good value.
🧺 *Widely available.*

★★½ **2002 Wyndham Estate Bin 222 Chardonnay**
$14-15
Good value, medium-bodied quaffing chardonnay for everyday pleasure. It's light in fruit flavour but has loads of appealing creamy texture and body.
🧺 *Widely available.*

★★★ **2001 Wynns Coonawarra Estate Chardonnay**
$17-18
A classic Aussie chardonnay under $20, big and creamy with strong spicy oak flavours at least as predominant as the fruit. This is a reliable, if slightly over-the-top, style of wine and good value for everyday drinking.
🧺 *Widely available.*

★★★ **2001 Yalumba Barossa Chardonnay**
$16-17
Lovely fresh, pure grapey-tasting wine without the affectation of too much oak. Medium weight and good length of flavour. Offers fantastic value for money.
🧺 *Specialist wine stores.*

★★ **2002 Yalumba Oxford Landing Chardonnay**
$12-13 Green, sappy, soapy wine without much to commend it. A bit sickly and sweet-tasting.
🛒 *New World, Pak 'N Save, specialist wine stores.*

★★½ **2002 Yalumba Y Unwooded Chardonnay**
$15-16 Light and fresh with a hint of green-herb flavour, which might just make it work well with lightly pan-fried fresh fish squeezed with lemon. Good value for money for such an honest wine, offering purity of flavour.
🛒 *Specialist wine stores.*

CHENIN BLANC

Chenin blanc was once a workhorse grape of the New Zealand wine industry, but its plantings are slowly shrinking and currently sit at a relatively small 129 hectares nationwide.
It is also known as Pineau or Pineau de la Loire, in France, its spiritual home and, although usually under-valued, chenin blanc can make long-lived dessert wines of high quality in France.
Chenin blanc is one of the main grapes grown in South Africa, with variable results.

★★★ **2002 Collards Hawke's Bay Chenin Blanc**
$12-14

Good value warm, fresh white made from the little known chenin blanc grape, which comes originally from France's Loire Valley where it is highly prized for its appley freshness. This wine has exactly that quality, too, and a highly affordable price tag. Buy half a case and love it in the sunshine, or pre-dinner in winter. Medium-bodied with a lingering flavour.

👑 *Widely available, or from Collards winery, phone (09) 838 8341.*

★★ **2002 Collards Summerfields Chenin Sauvignon Chardonnay**
$7-9

A very light, very simple white blend of the three grape varieties – chenin blanc, sauvignon blanc and chardonnay. This is a tad green in flavour and on the finish but clean and fresh, providing good basic plonk for everyday summer drinking.

👑 *Widely available, or from Collards winery, phone (09) 838 8341.*

★★ **1999 KWV Chenin Blanc**
$10-11

For decades South Africa's wine industry has been built around the often-innocuous white made from chenin blanc grapes. Today there is more to South African wine than these light whites, but this is a very fresh, summery white wine with zest and zing, making it a good food wine.

👑 *Liquor stores and supermarkets, or contact Federal Geo for stockists, phone (09) 578 1823, email: federalgeo@xtra.co.nz*

★★½ **2001 Robert's Rock Chenin Chardonnay**
$12-13 This is a pretty plain white wine made by blending chenin blanc grapes with chardonnay. The chardonnay adds body to this lightish style.

🛒 *Liquor stores, or contact Federal Geo for stockists, phone (09) 578 1823, email: federalgeo@xtra.co.nz*

GEWÜRZTRAMINER

Gewürztraminer is a mutation of the traminer grape variety, which originates in the Italian village of Tramin or Termeno (now the Italian Tyrol). It can be a difficult grape to grow, because it is a sensitive, wind- and frost-prone grape variety, and yet produces the most interesting flavours when grown in a relatively cool climate.

New Zealand's plantings of gewürztraminer are slowly increasing and grew over the last year from 178 to 212 hectares today. The numbers are small, but in percentage terms this is an enormous leap with predictions for an increase of 39 percent in gewürztraminer planted in New Zealand between 2003 and 2005, according to the *New Zealand Grape and Wine Industry Statistical Annual 2002*. This is good news for lovers of highly aromatic, high-quality wines, and the taste and quality of locally produced gewürz (as it is often abbreviated to) has also improved over the last year.

The best gewürztraminers come from coolish-climate wine-producing regions such as Alsace in northern France and some parts of Germany.

It is not hard to say:
gewürztraminer = give-urts-tram-een-er.

★★★½ 2002 Burnt Spur Gewürztraminer
$20

Burnt Spur is a new winery on the Martinborough scene, making some fantastic and bone-dry wines with intense limey flavours and such finesse. Brilliant! Higher price offerings from the Spur soon will be viognier and syrah.

Contact Federal Geo for stockists, phone (09) 578 1823, email: federalgeo@xtra.co.nz

★★★★ 2002 Collards Hawke's Bay Gewürztraminer
$15-17

STAR BUY

Yellow with a hint of pink colour and a gorgeous rose aroma penetrating the nose. Nice robust acids stretch out the rose-petal, classic, Turkish delight flavours here.

Widely available.

★★★ 2002 Crossroads Hawke's Bay Destination Series Gewürztraminer
$19-20

Rose-petally, Turkish-delight-tasting gewürz with lovely spicy flavours, medium weight and a nice medium length.

Widely available.

★★ 2002 Huntaway Reserve Gewürztraminer
$19-20

Made from grapes grown in Gisborne and Marlborough, and it tastes green gingery, with a sour and dulled fruit flavour.

Liquor stores and specialist wine stores.

★★★ 2002 Hunter's Marlborough Gewürztraminer
$19-20

Another lovely gewürztraminer, this time made from grapes grown in Marlborough. This wine smells like freshly made, soft Turkish delight with a fresh dusting of icing sugar.

Specialist wine stores, or Hunter's Wines, phone (03) 572 8489.

★★½ 2002 Kaikoura Marlborough Gewürztraminer
$17-18

This Marlborough-grown, Kaikoura-produced wine has a hugely attractive floral nose. It smells of rose petals and that's the flavour too – freshly picked rose petals, of course. It's the sort of wine that inspires thoughts of lovely spicy, rosy and lychee flavours. Deliciously intense in flavour but lithe in texture and smooth with a medium-to-long finish.

🛒 Specialist wine stores, or Kaikoura Wine Company, phone (03) 319 4440, email: Kaikoura.wines@xtra.co.nz or www.kaikourawines.co.nz

★★½ 2002 Kemblefield The Distinction Gewürztraminer
$19-20

If you see a flash of pink colour in this spicy-tasting, light, fresh aromatic white, don't be surprised. Gewürztraminer grapes are pinkish when ripe, and this wine is certainly made from ripe grapes, which have hints of that hallmark gewürzy rose flavour.

🛒 Fine Wine Delivery Company, Auckland; Havelock Wines & Spirits; Moore Wilson and New World, Thorndon, Wellington; or from the winery, phone (06) 874 9649, email: kew@kemblefield.co.nz

★★ 2002 Longridge Vineyards Gewürztraminer
$14-15

Has a very light, pretty, aromatic thing happening on the nose, but palate-wise it's pretty basic, showing predominantly a simple oaky-type flavour. Less than satisfying, with the acids adding the only real balance here.

🛒 Widely available.

★★★ 2002 Mills Reef Reserve Gewürztraminer
$19-20

The first whiff of this wine says yum! It smells and tastes like Turkish delight. Fantastic value for money to get this sort of concentration and pure gewürz flavour without being cloying. It doesn't linger at the finish but has a lovely balance of acids adding life and zest.

🧺 *Widely available in supermarkets and wine stores nationwide, or contact Mills Reef Winery, phone (07) 576 8800.*

★★½ 2002 Mission Estate Hawke's Bay Gewürztraminer
$14-16

A very light and pretty gewürztraminer without the intensity of some of the others here, but in some ways that makes it more palatable in its fresh, zingy, lightly spicy style. This wine offers lots of value.

🧺 *Widely available, or from Mission Estate Winery, phone (06) 844 2259.*

★★★ 2002 Saints Vineyard Selection Gisborne Gewürztraminer
$16-17

Lovely soft-textured Gisborne gewürztraminer, lacking intensity of flavour but showing some pleasant varietal purity. The finish is a little short but that is my only real gripe. Otherwise this is a deliciously easy-to-like wine.

🧺 *Widely available.*

★★★½ 2002 Seifried Estate Gewürztraminer
$18-19

Newly released when tasted. Sealed with a screwcap, which allows the wine to be itself. It is very spicy and rosy in aroma and flavour, offering lots of rose-petally, spicy gewürz flavours that are nicely balanced. Fantastic stuff, if you're a spice fan.

🧺 *Widely available.*

★★★ **2001 Seifried Estate Winemaker's Collection**
$19-20 **Dry Gewürztraminer**
A refreshingly dry gewürztraminer made by Austrian-born winemaker Hermann Seifried from grapes grown in Nelson. This is great value and very good quality wine with all the classic rose-petal, lychee aromas and a far drier end-taste than most gewürztraminers in New Zealand.
Widely available.

★★★½ **2002 Spy Valley Marlborough Gewürztraminer**
$18-19 Fresh but with very high alcohol – 14 percent. Has lovely Turkish delight and marshmallow flavour and intensity, and beautiful soft, smooth texture, but boy it's a heady little number!
Specialist wine stores.

★★★ **2001 Taylors Estate Gewürztraminer**
$16-17 Very light but clean and fresh wine in a vibrant new style.
Widely available.

★★★ **2002 Villa Maria Private Bin Gewürztraminer**
$17-18 Lightish style with the aromas and hints of Turkish delight flavour ending on a vibrant note of zingy acids, stretching out the floral rosy flavours to a lingering finish.
Widely available.

MÜLLER-THURGAU

The müller-thurgau grape is a German cross of two grapes, riesling and silvaner, and was developed by the Swiss-born Dr Hermann Müller in 1882. Until 1993 it was New Zealand's most planted grape variety, but the country's national vineyard area devoted to müller-thurgau has now declined from 1,109 hectares in 1993 to just 342 hectares nationally today, largely in favour of the far more quality-oriented chardonnay, which also lends itself to a drier style of wine, in keeping with the nation's continually evolving wine tastes. Müller-thurgau is also known as riesling-sylvaner in New Zealand and Switzerland, as rivaner in Luxembourg and Slovenia, and as rizlingszilvani in Hungary.

★★½ **2002 Corbans White Label Müller-Thurgau**
$8-9

True to type with a light, fresh floral aroma and flavour, more pleasing on the nose than the palate, where it is a little dilute and light, but if you like this aromatic fresh style, then this is good value at this price.

🧺 *Widely available.*

★★ **Jackman Ridge Müller-Thurgau**
$8-9 Smells a little dirty and, although it is attractively sweet and aromatic, it is extremely light and thin. Lolly-waterish but inoffensive.

🧺 *Widely available.*

★ **Wohnsiedler Müller-Thurgau**
$6-7 Non-vintage wine. It's hard to believe I fell in love with wine because of this particular wine, which has virtually no flavour, dulled fruitiness and a vague lolly-water character.

🧺 *Widely available.*

OTHER WHITE WINES AND BRANDED WHITES

If you want to know more about some of the quirkiest white wines in the world, then you really need to read the fantastically priced little pocket guide, *Jancis Robinson's Guide to Wine Grapes*. This is packed with information on all of the well-known grapes and wines as well as the weird and wonderful grape varieties in the world, like verdicchio, sylvaner and muscadet, all of which feature in this chapter.

AUSTRALIA

★★★½ **2002 Cockfighter's Ghost Hunter Valley**
$18-19 **Verdelho**
Peachy, fresh white wine with spicy, lovely flavours and medium weight and length. Great value and a great, unoaked, fresh-tasting alternative to the ever-present chardonnay.
🛒 *Specialist wine stores, or contact Macvine, phone (03) 570 2118.*

★★★ **2002 Houghton White Burgundy**
$12-13 Lovely aromatic and light white, which makes great summer drinking in the sun, especially if you serve this wine just lightly chilled. And while it's aromatic, this is not cloying or sweet but rather a medium-dry style. Excellent stuff, delivering flavour as well as value.
🛒 *Widely available.*

FRANCE

★★★ **2000 Domaine de la Cognardiere Muscadet**
$13-14 Here is a wine that tastes like wine. No, really. It just has that fresh, grapey flavour with a kick of alcohol aiding its appeal and a hint of creamy texture stretching out its length. Great stuff for summer daytime drinking, especially with shellfish.
🛒 *Chateauneuf store, 48 Pollen Street, Ponsonby, Auckland; or by mail order, phone (09) 378 7011, email: Chateauneuf@xtra.co.nz*

2000 Henri Erhart Sylvaner Vin d'Alsace

★★ $15-16

Very simple white from Alsace in north-west France. This wine has a creamy texture but very plain character. Basic quaffing.

♛ *Chateauneuf store, 48 Pollen Street, Ponsonby, Auckland; or by mail order, phone (09) 378 7011, email: Chateauneuf@xtra.co.nz*

ITALY

2001 Ca Montini Soave

★★★ $15-16

Lovely white Italian wine with gorgeously fresh flavours verging on almonds and grapes and a touch of grapefruitiness about it. Great value at this price. Good alternative to chardonnay too.

♛ *Specialist wine stores, or contact importer Phil Clark at A Touch of Italy for more information, phone (09) 273 3701, email: sales@touchofitaly.co.nz*

2001 Duca de Castelmonte Fiorile Grecanico

★★½ $12-13

This fresh-tasting Italian white is a little on the plain side but clean and light so that it is good summer daytime drinking.

♛ *Specialist wine stores, or contact importer Phil Clark at A Touch of Italy for more information, phone (09) 273 3701, email: sales@touchofitaly.co.nz*

1999 Pasqua Soave Classico

★★★ $12-13

Lovely light Italian white. If you find it a little austere, make some pasta with your favourite creamy sauce and top with roasted pumpkin and parmesan. Then you will taste this wine really coming into its fresh, spicy own.

♛ *Glengarry, North Island.*

★★ **2001 Renzo Masi Bianco Vergine Valdichiana**
$13-14
Slightly rustic Italian white, which is best consumed with a bowl of light vegetable-based pasta and parmagiano. Very light in body and flavour, average value for money.
🛒 *Specialist wine stores, or contact importer Phil Clark at A Touch of Italy for more information, phone (09) 273 3701, email: sales@touchofitaly.co.nz*

★★★ **2001 Umani Ronchi Villa Bianchi Verdicchio**
$15-16
This verdicchio is a lovely soft and creamy white with surprisingly impressive textural qualities and medium body.

🛒 *Specialist wine stores, or contact Vintners New Zealand for stockists near you, phone (09) 979 2900, email: enquiries@vintnersnz.co.nz*

NEW ZEALAND

★★½ **Nobilo White Cloud**
$8-9
This famous New Zealand wine brand with fantastic export success is declared to be a medium style of wine on the front label. In aroma it is light but the palate is sweet and fruity with fresh, light floral flavours. Good value for money too.
🛒 *Widely available.*

★★½ 2002 Rippon Vineyard Ralph Hotere White Wine
$14-15

Love the label of this anonymous blend of white grape varieties, fermented dry to finish an aromatic, light-bodied wine with a fresh zing. Lovely in the sunshine. Love to know the identity of the varieties of this, one of the world's most southern wines.

🛒 *Centre City New World, Wellington; Liquor King, Dunedin; Fresh Choice, Queenstown; New World, Mosgiel; and at Rippon Vineyard, Mount Aspiring Road, Wanaka, phone (03) 443 8084, email: rippon@xtra.co.nz*

★½ St Aubyns Dry White Wine
$7-8

Slightly dirty-tasting white with a dryish finish but slightly woody flavours coming through, which is interesting given that this is one of the few wines to come out of the vast Villa Maria winery, New Zealand's third biggest, without a screwcap.

🛒 *Widely available.*

★★ St Aubyns Medium White Wine
$7-8

Fresh and lightly aromatic wine which has both feet in the medium camp; the finish on this wine is medium rather than sweet, as the word 'medium' sometimes suggests. And it is an easy-to-enjoy white while sitting in the sun.

🛒 *Widely available.*

PINOT GRIS

For years the New Zealand wine industry has been touting pinot gris as 'The Next Big Thing'. At the same time, plantings of this mutant pinot noir grape have grown slightly, and consumption has grown in tandem with the subsequent growth in production, much of which is due to enormous press attention to this dry white wine, which is constantly touted as a good alternative to chardonnay.

The wines in this chapter come from New Zealand, Australia, Italy, France and Argentina. And like their varied origins, the quality and style ranges widely from impressive aromatic whites with full body and long, lingering flavours to light and relatively plain. When pinot gris grapes are growing, they are often mistaken for pinot noir, because their vines have identical leaves, and it is common to find pinot gris growing among some of France's most prized pinot noir vines in Burgundy, the spiritual home of pinot noir.

Pinot gris is also known as malvoisie in Switzerland, tokay in Alsace, France, and as rulander and as grauburgunder in Germany.

★★★ 2002 Babich Marlborough Pinot Gris
$14-15

If pinot gris really is 'The Next Big Thing', then this wine will be among the leaders. It's a commercial style, made in relatively large quantities, but it doesn't sacrifice style or flavour in its peary, crisp character. Good value for money. And it's especially good served chilled.

🧺 *Widely available.*

★★★★ 2002 Bodega Lurton Pinot Gris
$17-18
STAR BUY

'Wow' is hardly descriptive, but it's the first impression most wine drinkers have of this sensational wine, which is made in Argentina by French flying winemakers Jacques and François Lurton. There are all the textural qualities of grainy mouthful, lingering finish and spicy, pear-like flavours but lots more too. This is fantastic value for money, buy as much as you can!

🧺 *Specialist wine stores, or contact Bennett & Deller Wine Merchants for stores near you, phone (09) 378 9463.*

★½ 2002 Corbans Pinot Gris
$13-14

This is a light, thin-tasting wine, and even at this price it is not representative of what good pinot gris is about.

🧺 *Widely available.*

★★ 2002 Danzante Pinot Grigio
$19-20

Light and relatively lacklustre white with vaguely grapey flavours and a short finish.

🧺 *Foodtown, New World, Woolworths, specialist wine stores.*

★★★ **2002 Drylands Marlborough Pinot Gris**
$18-19
Lovely fresh pinot gris made with grapes grown in Marlborough, which give this wine an unctuous, oily texture and tasty dry finish. Good value.
🛒 Widely available.

★★★½ **2000 W Gisselbrecht Tokay Pinot Gris**
$17-18 **Vin D'Alsace**
This Alsatian pinot gris has flavours of honey but is not at all over-the-top, with beautifully balanced, bright, strong acids at the front countered with spicy, fruity flavours at the finish.
🛒 Glengarry, North Island; or contact Paul Sharp for more information, phone (09) 379 3740.

★★★ **2002 Gladstone Wairarapa Pinot Gris**
$18-19
Gladstone winery is a jewel tucked into the heat-filled Wairarapa's crown. You need to get off the beaten track to find it and its fresh, lively wines like this peary-tasting pinot gris. This is a light white wine with hints of spicy tastes and a soft texture. It is also a very good food wine – its grapey flavours will not fight with most white meats and they will work deliciously well with roasted pork or chicken smeared in your favourite spices.
🛒 Gladstone Vineyard, phone (06) 379 8563.

★★★ 2001 Henri Ehrhart Tokay Pinot Gris Vin D'Alsace
$14-15

From Chateauneuf in Auckland. Great stuff, especially at this particular price. Honeyed and smooth but still young enough to be enjoyed dryish to medium, especially with Chinese food such as unctuously coated fish or chicken. Very food-friendly.

Chateauneuf store, 48 Pollen Street, Ponsonby, Auckland; or by mail order, phone (09) 378 7011, email: Chateauneuf@xtra.co.nz

★★ 2002 Huntaway Reserve Marlborough Pinot Gris
$19-20

It might say reserve on the label but there is no non-reserve wine in the Huntaway stable. This affordable pinot gris is light and a little lean in taste with hints of greenness and Granny Smith apple-like acids. Average.

Liquor stores and specialist wine stores.

★★½ 2002 Kim Crawford Boyszone Vineyard Marlborough Pinot Gris
$19-20

This 'Boyszone' pinot gris has clean, fresh pear-like flavours and a suave, light texture.

Glengarry, North Island; specialist wine stores nationwide.

★★ 2001 Mezza Corona Pinot Grigio
$19-20

This is a relatively light, slightly gingery-tasting Italian white. Its finish is slightly sour and at this price it is not good value for money.

Specialist wine stores, or contact importer Phil Clark at A Touch of Italy for more information, phone (09) 273 3701, email: sales@touchofitaly.co.nz

★★ **2002 Mission Estate Hawke's Bay Pinot Gris**
$14-16 A creamy-flavoured wine with a slightly plain, short finish. Not great.
  🍷 *Widely available, or from Mission Estate Winery, phone (06) 844 2259.*

★★★ **2002 Redbank Sunday Morning Pinot Gris**
$19-20 I love the evocative name of this wine, which perfectly fits the notion of a light, fresh style of wine to drink late Sunday morning. This is a vibrant, zesty pinot gris with hard-to-pin-down flavours and a zingy lively style that tastes fresh with every mouthful.
  🍷 *Specialist wine stores.*

★★½ **2002 Saint Clair Marlborough Pinot Gris**
$17-18 Fresh peary-tasting pinot gris, with a lovely spicy style, clean, very refreshing flavour and excellent length. Delicious.
  🍷 *Widely available.*

★★★ **2002 St Helena Canterbury Pinot Gris**
$14-15 A scrumptious light pinot gris with flavours of fresh white pear and a medium finish. Good value, lovely drinking.
  🍷 *Widely available.*

★★½ **2002 Shingle Peak Pinot Gris**
$18-19 This evocatively illustrated label is the South Island face for Matua Valley Wines, based in West Auckland. It's a light style of pinot gris with notes of spice, pear and apple flavours in a smooth-textured white.
  🍷 *Widely available.*

★★★½ **2002 Spy Valley Marlborough Pinot Gris**
$19-20 This lovely intense zingy pinot gris has more flavour than many on the New Zealand market, showing that this country can produce bone-dry, texturally driven and very stylish pinot gris. Like the best from Alsace, France, this one has flavours that are hard to define, hinting at fruitiness with tastes of pear and even peaches on the finish.
Specialist wine stores.

★★½ **2002 Tasman Bay Nelson Pinot Gris**
$17-18 Nelson based winemakers Phil Jones and Matthew Rutherford use grapes grown in Marlborough to make this fresh, high-acid pinot gris. It tastes young in flavour and relatively acidic on its slightly biting finish. Best to drink with food.
Widely available.

RIESLING

The mere mention of the word 'riesling' is enough to send most wine-lovers running to the nearest chardonnay shelf, which is a pity because riesling makes some of the world's greatest white wines. They range from bone-dry, lime-tasting creatures from Alsace, France; the Rhine River, Germany; and Australia's coolest winemaking regions, through to intense-tasting, light but flavoursome, low-alcohol German wines from the Mosel-Saar-Ruwer rivers. New Zealand also makes some top-notch rieslings in dry, medium and sweet, dessert-wine styles. The riesling vine is particularly hardy, making it a good choice for cool-climate grape-growing regions, like many of New Zealand's, where it can ripen gradually over a long period of time.

★★★ 2002 Alana Estate Riesling
$17-18

This wine tastes just as delicious now as when I first tasted it at the brand new Alana Estate winery in Martinborough, at one of that region's wine and food festivals about seven years ago. Winemaker Christian Ullrich has allowed this wine's intense floral aromas and flavours to speak for themselves in this well-balanced, incredibly tasty riesling, which also happens to be one of the most affordable wines made in Martinborough.

Specialist wine stores; or contact Alana Estate, phone (06) 306 9784.

★★★ 2002 Ascension Vineyard Marlborough Riesling
$19-20

Darryl Soljan planted his Matakana vineyard in 1996 with grapes he believes are suited to the region, which does not include riesling – his grapes in this wine come from Marlborough. The riesling is a lovely floral wine with a lightish body and style, jasmine-like but very light and a little short, although it finishes on a decently dry note. I like it.

Specialist wine stores.

★★★★ 2002 Babich Riesling
$14-16

Fantastic stuff, this Marlborough riesling. And if you like it now, you'll love it after a couple of years, because this fresh, clean, lime- and jasmine-tasting riesling improves out of sight after a couple of years. Then again, it tastes so good now, why wait? Team it up with some friends and seafood.

Widely available.

★★★½ **2002 Burnt Spur Riesling**
$19-20

Burnt Spur is a new winery on the Martinborough scene, making this fantastically bone-dry riesling with its intense limey flavours and such finesse. Brilliant. Higher priced offerings from the Spur will soon see viognier and syrah out under this newish label.

Specialist wine stores, or contact Burnt Spur Martinborough, phone (06) 306 9174.

★★★ **2001 Cairnbrae Old River Marlborough Riesling**
$18-19

Winemaker Tony Bish describes this Marlborough riesling as medium to dry in style. It is also a relatively light-tasting wine with sweetish grapefruity flavours and a crisp finish. Good summer drinking but just average value, at this price.

Specialist wine stores, or contact Cairnbrae Vineyards phone (03) 572 8018, email: info@cairnbrae.co.nz

★★½ **2002 Clifford Bay Riesling**
$16-17

Youthful, vibrant wine with big acids and lots of aromatic lime and orange flavours but a little bitter at the finish. Shows fantastic potential for Marlborough riesling, but needs to do better…

Most supermarkets and specialist wine stores.

★★★ **2002 Coopers Creek Marlborough Riesling**
$15-16

Here is one of the many New Zealand rieslings that demonstrate the potential of riesling in this country but are not quite there. It has lovely floral fresh style but the green gingery finish is masking unripeness. It needs to be riper for balance but it has hints and flashes of greatness.

Foodtown supermarkets and most wine stores.

★★
$13-14

2002 Corbans Marlborough Riesling
Nice label – stylish and very New Zealandish. The wine itself is a bit of a disappointment, with flat flavours. This is a shame, given the high quality of the next wine.
🧺 *Widely available.*

★★★½
$8-9

2002 Corbans White Label Johannisburg Riesling
If there was space to champion the best white wine under $10, this delicious light riesling would win hands down. Every year it has a consistently pure varietal riesling aroma and a flavour of jasmine and dried orange peel with hints of cloves, orange and spice. Light to medium in style, it is fantastic value for money.
🧺 *Widely available.*

★★½
$19-20

2002 Crossroads Hawke's Bay Destination Series Riesling
Light, fresh riesling; the least impressive of the whites in this series but still nice and tasty. Probably only worth about $16 because, although it is fresh and clean, it lacks concentration of flavour just a tad.
🧺 *Widely available.*

★★★½
$18-19

2002 Drylands Marlborough Dry Riesling
This unabashedly dry style of riesling takes you by complete surprise with its initially austere flavours but, all of a sudden mid-palate, it comes on all succulent and fresh. The finish is long and this is very good value for money. Team it up with shellfish and lime.
🧺 *Widely available.*

★★★★
$19-20
STAR BUY

2002 Esk Valley Hawke's Bay Riesling
Deliciously floral, pineapple flavours intermingle in an unbelievably fresh take on riesling, and the screwcap allows this wine to show just what it should be – pure and unadulterated by the random flavours that cork can impart. Fantastic stuff.
🛒 *Widely available.*

★★
$16-17

2002 Giesen Canterbury/Marlborough Riesling
A tad bitter in flavour but has some lovely floral aromas and zingy acids. Needs time to soften out, and I think it would benefit from being made from Marlborough grapes only.
🛒 *Fine Wine Delivery Company and Wine Masters, Auckland; Woolworths; Liquorland; or contact Burleigh Trading for more stockists, phone (09) 480 0789.*

★★★
$17-18

2000 W Gisselbrecht Riesling Vin D'Alsace
This fantastic-value French riesling has zingy acids on the front palate leading into a mouthful of fresh apple flavour and is deliciously long in finish. Perfect for drinking with shellfish and panfried fresh prawns with garlic, ginger, coriander and chilli.
🛒 *Glengarry, North Island; or contact Paul Sharp, phone (09) 379 3740.*

★★½
$15-16

2002 Goldridge Estate Hawke's Bay Riesling
This wine is made from grapes grown in Hawke's Bay but packaged under the Matakana label, Goldridge Estate. It's a medium style with a noticeable sweetness at the front of each mouthful followed by a light-bodied style. Serve it chilled. This is clean, fresh riesling but a little light, so is average value for money.
🛒 *Widely available in specialist wine stores and liquor retailers.*

★★★½ **2002 Greenhough Nelson Riesling**
$18-19
Bright green fresh new Nelson riesling, which is incredibly zingy and vibrant – sealed with its screwcap, which appears to keep in all its flavours.

🍷 *Specialist wine stores, or Greenhough Vineyard and Winery, phone (03) 542 3868.*

★★★ **2002 Grove Mill Riesling**
$18-19
I love the varietal purity of this wine; it really smells and tastes like riesling with its limey freshness and appley flavours. Great value for money and too easy to drink.

🍷 *Most supermarkets and some specialist wine stores, or contact the winery, phone (03) 572 8200, email: info@grovemill.co.nz*

★★ **2002 Hunter's Estate White Riesling Sauvignon Blanc**
$14-15
A strange combination that doesn't work brilliantly well because of the intermingling of two strongly flavoured aromatic grape varieties, neither of which is able to shine in this mix. Drink it chilled on a bright summer day, relaxing on the lawn.

🍷 *Hunter's Wines, phone (03) 572 8489.*

★★½ **2002 Hunter's Marlborough Riesling**
$16-17
This Marlborough riesling has relatively high acids balanced by light, fresh, floral flavours. It is a tad green on the finish.

🍷 *Specialist wine stores, or Hunter's Wines, phone (03) 572 8489.*

★★★ 2002 Hunter's Marlborough Riesling
$18-19

This lively young riesling made from grapes grown in Marlborough tastes incredibly youthful and zingy. It's deliciously fresh but will evolve to develop more pronounced floral and sweet orange flavours over the next couple of years. Drink now if you like riesling to taste fresh and slightly austere, or else buy a case and watch it develop. Good value.

Specialist wine stores, or Hunter's Wines, phone (03) 572 8489.

★★★½ 2002 Jacob's Creek Reserve Riesling
$11-12

This lovable, big-name wine has a just off-dry style and sweet lemon and lime flavours. It's a great introduction to riesling for those who are still not convinced this is one of the greatest white wines in the world. And at this price, it's fantastic value.

Widely available.

★★★ 2000 Jean Greiner Riesling
$18-19

A lovely fresh, dry riesling with a slightly austere character that is limey and zingy. Excellent value for money for a classic Alsatian white that would be perfect with fresh fish.

Macvine, phone (03) 570 2118, email: Macvine@voyager.co.nz

★★★ 2001 Johanneshof Marlborough Riesling
$17-18

Zingy and intensely apple-tasting Marlborough riesling with light characteristics giving it freshness and an impressive long length of flavour at the finish of each mouthful. Good buying.

Specialist wine stores.

★★½ 2002 Kaikoura Canterbury Riesling
$16-18

Lest you are ever so slightly confused, this wine is made with grapes grown in Canterbury but processed into wine at the Kaikoura Winery slightly south of there, on the stunning, rugged coastline. It is a medium-style wine with a light body and sweetish finish, with flavours of orange peel and spice. Okay value.

Specialist wine stores.

★★★½ 1995 Karthauser Eitelsbacher
$19-20

One of the most appealing features of wines like this German riesling is the refreshing, relatively low 10 percent alcohol it contains. This is made from grapes grown along the Mosel River in Germany, which is renowned for producing minerally, light, succulent rieslings with floral aromas and a crisp, strong acid finish. Fantastic value for money.

Specialist wine stores, or contact Wine Direct for a store near you, or for mail order, freephone 0800 660 777.

★★★ 2002 Kim Crawford Marlborough Dry Riesling
$19-20

Very good value riesling made by winemaker Kim Crawford. And although it is relentlessly dry, this is a hugely friendly style of riesling with ripe, sweet appley flavours and a long, well-balanced finish. Good buying.

Glengarry, North Island; specialist wine stores nationwide.

★★★½ **2001 Knappstein Clare Valley Riesling**
$19-20

This is quality Australian riesling from the relatively cool climate of the Clare Valley. It tastes dry and fresh with a hint of limey flavour and the definitive crispness that gives dry riesling all of its allure. This is great value for money. The grapes in the wine were hand-picked to ensure quality – as the label states – and it is sealed with a screwcap to further ensure freshness.

🛒 Liquor King and specialist wine stores.

★★★½ **2002 Lake Chalice Falcon Vineyard Riesling**
$17-18

Whoever says that screwcaps can't look good obviously has not taken a squiz at this fabulously elegant, chrome look-alike seal, which is only just noticeably not a foil seal up close. It's also a gorgeous wine with lovely fresh jasmine aromas and flavours of orange peel and cloves, and has gorgeous long length and medium weight. Fantastic wine, so drinkable in the sunshine. Full of character and fresh flavour, a wine with personality.

🛒 Glengarry and some other specialist wine stores, or Lake Chalice Wines, phone (03) 572 9327, email: wine@lakechalice.co.nz

★★ **2002 Lucknow Estate Waihopai Valley Riesling**
$17-18

A lean style of riesling with fresh flavours, but it's a bit grippy at the finish.

🛒 New World, Lower Hutt and Wellington; and from Lucknow Estate, phone (06) 874 9007, email: lucknow@xtra.co.nz

★★★ **2001 Main Divide Canterbury Riesling**
$14-16

Love the name and the wine. For mainlanders – those of us born south of the Cook Strait on New Zealand's South Island – main divide has a special meaning, but it's clear that even though there is a divide between this label and that of Pegasus Bay's other wines, this is a darling little riesling with hints of honey, ginger and clove flavours and a light, balanced style. Delicious stuff and a great price.

🛒 *Specialist wine stores, or Pegasus Bay Winery, phone (03) 314 6869.*

★★ **2002 Mills Reef Reserve Riesling**
$16-17

The Tauranga-based winery that makes this fresh aromatic floral riesling gets its grapes from all over – Hawke's Bay in this case. This wine is a tad green gingery on the finish, making it good with Asian-styled food but not much chop on its own.

🛒 *Widely available in supermarkets, wine stores nationwide, or contact Mills Reef Winery, phone (07) 576 8800.*

★★½ **2000 Mills Reef Riesling**
$14-15

This is the lower priced of the two rieslings from this Tauranga-based winery at Katikati and is actually the more pleasant wine. It's lighter and fresher with a pretty short finish but good after-work quaffing, served chilled.

🛒 *Widely available in supermarkets, wine stores nationwide, or contact Mills Reef Winery, phone (07) 576 8800.*

★★½
$14-16

2002 Mission Estate Hawke's Bay Riesling

Like most rieslings from the Bay, this one is fresh and clean but lighter in flavour than many of its southern counterparts. There is a flash of Granny Smith apples and a hint of lime in this wine, and it has a very appealing price tag. Average value for the flavour it offers.

Widely available, or from Mission Estate Winery, phone (06) 844 2259.

★★★
$19-20

2001 Mitchelton Blackwood Park Riesling

Zingy little Australian riesling with fresh flavours and a developed honey flavour. Medium body and length.

Liquor King and specialist wine stores.

★★★
$14-15

2002 Montana Marlborough Riesling

Lovely easy-to-like riesling with a touch of green and relatively high residual sugar giving its less than fully ripe grapes drinkability.

Widely available.

★★★
$19-20

2001 Montana Reserve Marlborough Vintage Release Riesling

This is one of those wines that sneaks up on you with refreshingly dry riesling characters like dry lime flavours and a long, lingering finish. It's made from grapes grown in Marlborough and is very good value.

Widely available.

★★★½
$14-15

2002 Mount Riley Marlborough Riesling
A fresh, floral riesling that tastes excellent with lightly chilli, garlic, aromatic spicy foods, especially those with cumin-type flavours. This is dryish on the finish, which is refreshing – at least it seems to be dry. Again no residual sugar is given so it is impossible to know for sure.

Specialist wine stores, or contact the winery, email: john@mountriley.co.nz

★★½
$19-20

2002 Murdoch James Estate Riesling
This Martinborough wine is fresh and floral with a nice dry finish but a little bit light in style, making it refreshing for summer drinking.

Specialist wine stores, or Murdoch James Estate Wines, phone (03) 306 9165.

★½
$9-10

2002 Murray Ridge Riesling
Very basic riesling with a slightly grippy finish.

Widely available.

★★★½
$19-20

2002 Neudorf Brightwater Riesling
It's not just the name – this wine really does seem brighter in style sealed, as this vintage is, with a screwcap which allows its clean, floral and apple fresh flavours to shine through.

Specialist wine stores, or Neudorf Vineyards, phone (03) 543 2643.

★★★½ 2002 Neudorf Moutere Riesling
$18-20

Gorgeous floral riesling style; I love the alcohol erring on the low side too. Stylish but incredibly young and needs time – both in the glass and the bottle. Seems a tad sulphury at the moment, so decanting is a must for this refined, elegant, Germanic-styled riesling from the clay soils in Nelson's Moutere Hills.

Specialist wine stores.

★★★★ 2001 Orlando St Helga Eden Valley Riesling
$19-20

I love this crisp, limey-tasting and refreshingly dry style of riesling, which is the norm for most Australian winemakers of riesling but a style departure for New Zealand. It's fantastic with shellfish and seafood but easy to enjoy the zingy flavours and appealing soft texture even on its own. Sealed with a screwcap.

Specialist wine stores.

★★½ 2002 Palliser Estate Martinborough Riesling
$18-20

Fresh, zingy riesling with greenish appley flavours. Average value for money.

Specialist wine stores, or Palliser Estate Wines, phone (06) 306 9019.

★★★ 2000 Queen Adelaide Riesling
$9-10

This wine falls easily into the drink-me-now category. Fill a glass and enjoy its limey, developed riesling flavours. The style starts out medium but finishes on a dry note, which is refreshing to drink and to know about at this price. Great value for money and surprisingly tasty.

Widely available.

★★½ 2002 Saint Clair Marlborough Riesling
$18-20

Fresh, clean and lively but a little light on the aromatics, which will develop as the wine grows older. But this is a drink-me-now style rather than a keep-me-and-wait.

🍷 *Widely available in supermarkets.*

★★½ 2002 St Helena South Island Riesling
$15-16

Lovely medium-style riesling led by its sweet floral and orange-peel flavours and aromas. Light but lovely summer drinking.

🍷 *Specialist wine stores, or St Helena Wines, phone (03) 323 8202.*

★★★ 2002 Sanctuary Marlborough Riesling
$14-15

A very appealing, medium-styled riesling with intense floral flavours.

🍷 *Most supermarkets and some specialist wine stores.*

★★★★ 2001 Seifried Estate Riesling
$17-18

Sealed with a screwcap for the first time and deliciously fresh and tasty. So light, it is a luscious, silky smooth, easy-to-love Nelson white. Fantastic value for money for one of the freshest, smoothest and finest whites on offer in New Zealand under $20. And just in case you were wondering, yes, the screwcap does appear to enhance the wine's fresh qualities and characters.

🍷 *Widely available.*

★★★ **2002 Selaks Marlborough Riesling**
$14-15 Here's a hugely appealing riesling with gorgeously aromatic flavours of sweet limes and tart apples. It finishes just a tad drying in style at the end of each mouthful, but that's a minor gripe for such a sensationally priced riesling. Perfect summer wine and great value for money.
Widely available.

★★★ **2002 Shingle Peak Marlborough Riesling**
$14-15 Lovely medium-styled riesling with some attractive residual sweet flavours balanced with incredibly fresh tastes of lime, Pacific Rose apples and a hint of spice at the finish. Would be very good with Asian flavours because it is soft and smooth. It goes without saying that with a three-star rating, this is fantastic value.
Widely available.

★★★ **2002 Spy Valley Marlborough Riesling**
$19-20 Lovely fresh, floral-tasting Marlborough riesling with youthful zing.
Specialist wine stores.

★★★½ **2002 Stoneleigh Marlborough Riesling**
$17-18 If you don't believe riesling is a great wine, then crack open a bottle of this sensationally fresh, lively little number made from grapes grown in Marlborough. It is one of the best rieslings in New Zealand each year, packed with floral fruity aromas and flavours like sweet orange, jasmine and cloves. And it improves in the bottle if you keep it flat on its back in a dark, cool place for a few years.
Widely available.

★★★½ 2002 Taylors Estate Clare Valley Riesling
$14-15

This wine is fresh and limey and has very good length of flavour, tasting of fresh, ripe sweet limes and crisp apples. Great value, excellent riesling in a dry style.

🛒 *Widely available.*

★★★ 2002 Thorn-Clarke Eden Valley Sandpiper Riesling
$19-20

Lovely lime flavours and firm, zingy acids combine here to make a fresh, bright riesling that is instantly drinkable and will unfold more aromatic flavours with time. Drink now if you like your rieslings austere and fresh, or hold it a while for a more flavoursome, floral number. Either way, this is good value for money.

🛒 *Specialist wine stores, or contact Burleigh Trading for stockists, phone (09) 480 0789.*

★★★ 2002 Timara Riesling
$9-10

Lovely floral and limey aromas in a sweet but highly appealing and true varietal expression of riesling. Great value.

🛒 *Widely available.*

★★★½ 2002 Trinity Hill Wairarapa Riesling
$16-17

A steely dry style with incredibly clean freshness, lovely fresh and surprising intensity of flavour with apples and limes and not a hint of any greenness in flavour. Fantastic wine and at this price it is nothing short of a steal.

🛒 *Widely available or contact the winery, phone (06) 879 7778, www.trinityhillwines.com*

★★★½   2002 Vidal Estate Marlborough Riesling
$17-18

Hawke's Bay winemaker Rod McDonald uses grapes from Marlborough's Wairau and Awatere valleys to make this stunning little riesling, which is a favourite at Vidal's winery restaurant. The wine is fresh-tasting with hints of lime flavour and medium style, which lifts and enhances the floral aromas and flavours without being at all cloying. Fantastically accessible in flavour and price.

🛒 *Widely available.*

★★★   2001 Villa Maria Cellar Selection Marlborough Riesling
$15-16

This is a fresh and citrusy-tasting riesling with relatively high acids, making it a good food wine with lingering flavours.

🛒 *Widely available.*

★★★   2002 Villa Maria Private Bin Riesling
$15-16

Textural appley riesling with lots of vibrant fresh flavours and a citrusy tang at the finish. This is summer in a glass.

🛒 *Widely available.*

★★★   2002 Waimea Estate Classic Riesling
$18-19

From one of the biggest wineries in Nelson at the often-forgotten north-east tip of the South Island. This fresh and intensely floral riesling takes you by surprise from the moment you have your first sensational sniff to the last sip. It's light-bodied and luscious in flavour, erring on the medium to sweet side.

🛒 *Liquor King, Liquorland and most supermarkets.*

★★★ 2002 Waimea Estate Dry Riesling
$19-20

Another very good riesling from the 2002 vintage of the vineyard that has turned out some of the best New Zealand rieslings in recent years – albeit in relatively small quantities. I like the dry finish on this crisp, fresh, slightly austere wine, which needs time to open up in flavour. Give it a year or two in the bottle for a more intensely flavoursome style or drink now to enjoy its fresh, youthful, lively riesling.

🛒 *Liquor King, Liquorland and most supermarkets.*

★★★ 1999 Willi Haag Riesling
$16-17

When you see the words Mosel-Saar-Ruwer on a German wine label, expect wines like this incredibly delicate riesling. It's medium to sweet in style but, surprisingly, incredibly refreshing, light and not at all cloying. Flavours are floral, lime and lemon.

🛒 *Specialist wine stores, or contact Wine Direct for a store near you or for mail order, freephone 0800 660 777.*

★★★½ 2002 Wolf Blass South Australia Riesling
$15-16

This luscious, limey riesling from South Australia has everything that is good about dry riesling styles. It's crisp and appley with lime-like tastes but nothing over-the-top here. This is beautifully balanced and fantastic value for money. And if you drink it with fresh prawns, stir fried with garlic, chilli and ginger you will have a marriage made in heaven.

🛒 *Widely available.*

★★ **2001 Woollaston Estates Riesling**
$17-19   Very lemon and lime riesling, youthful and fresh in character even at one year old, as at the time of tasting. It will improve with time but has fairly fierce acids, making it taste like lemon drops rather than rounded.

Seriously Fine Wines and St Helier's Wines, or mail order from Woollaston Estates winery, phone (03) 542 3205, email: wine@WoollastonEstates.co.nz

★★★ **2002 Yalumba South Australia Y Riesling**
$15-16   This nattily packaged wine with its stylish leaf on the top of the refreshingly modern label tastes all zingy and new. It is young and though lightish to medium in body it has very good intensity of lime taste and clean, long finish. Especially good at less than $20.

Specialist wine stores, or contact distributors Negociants New Zealand for more information, phone (09) 366 1140.

SAUVIGNON BLANC

The best sauvignon blancs from Marlborough, New Zealand, are widely regarded globally as unique because of the inimitable tropical array of flavours these wines boast: passionfruit, kiwifruit, gooseberry and even sweaty armpits (a compliment, believe it or not).

Sauvignon blanc is New Zealand's second most widely planted grape variety so it seems a little like bringing coals to Newcastle to have a range of imported wines featured in this chapter alongside our own. The best of the international bunch featured here do stand out above the rest because of their outgoing style and personality, and the others offer another type of quality in the form of subtlety and easy-going style.

Sauvignon blanc is generally a wine to drink young, and those that do age well – in the medium rather than the long term – tend to have either been fermented in or aged in oak. But even then they taste best consumed within the first two to three years of their life.

★★★ $14-16
2002 Babich Marlborough Sauvignon Blanc
This is a very herby-tasting Marlborough sauvignon with fruit flavours of gooseberry and kiwifruit and a slightly green finish. It's classic Marlborough savvy in the style that first made wine-lovers globally sit up and take notice of New Zealand wines.
Widely available.

★★★ $14-16
2002 Cairnbrae The Stones Sauvignon Blanc
Fresh, approachable, delicious daytime drink made from sauvignon blanc grapes grown, presumably on stony soils, in Marlborough. Great-value drinking.
Widely available.

★★½ $12-13
2002 Cat's Pee on a Gooseberry Bush Sauvignon Blanc
If it seems odd to award such a basic white a decent star rating then consider this: it's fresh and light and clean as a whistle; if it lacks intensity of flavour, the vibrant acids make it a good match with aromatic food without the heat of intense chilli. I like the cleanness and neutrality of this easy, honest quaffing style.
Glengarry, North Island; New World and Pak 'N Save.

★★½ $13-14
2001 Chateau de Garras Entre Deux Mers Sauvignon Sémillon
This French sauvignon and sémillon blended wine is in the mould of many New Zealand savvies with its grassy flavours and salty finish. Good with seafood but less intense than our local versions.
Chateauneuf store, 48 Pollen Street, Ponsonby, Auckland, or by mail order, phone (09) 378 7011, email: Chateauneuf@xtra.co.nz

★★★ **2002 Clifford Bay Sauvignon Blanc**
$16-17
Gains its appeal from a relatively high sweetness level that complements the fruit flavour of fresh gooseberries and kiwifruit nicely. Lingers at the finish and begs for strong citrusy-flavoured food to match the wine.
♛ *Most supermarkets and specialist wine stores.*

★★½ **2002 Coopers Creek Marlborough**
$15-16 **Sauvignon Blanc**
Very commercial style, typical for Marlborough with light, fresh flavours of gooseberries and kiwifruit but finishes a little sour and green and not particularly intense.
♛ *Foodtown, New World, Pak 'N Save, Woolworths, and most wine stores nationwide.*

★★ **2002 Corbans Sauvignon Blanc**
$13-14
A bit of a plain white wine with simple, light flavours and body. Basic.
♛ *Widely available.*

★★½ **2002 Corbans White Label Sauvignon Blanc**
$8-9
Lovely sauvignon blanc for the money with some intense flavours. Great value for more than average flavour and far above many other wines at this price.
♛ *Widely available.*

★★★½ **2002 Craggy Range Avery Vineyard**
$19-20 **Sauvignon Blanc**
The grapes in this wine are grown on vines that are 10 years old and this is the more subtle of the two Craggy Range sauvignons in this year's guide, with its savoury flavour and succulent texture. This is the sort of wine that takes you by surprise with its subtle and less-than-usual pungent immediacy.

Specialist wine stores, or Craggy Range Wines, phone (06) 877 7126, email: info@craggyrange.co.nz

★★★ **2002 Craggy Range Old Renwick Vineyard**
$19-20 **Sauvignon Blanc**
Rich, sweet gooseberry and passionfruit nose and an immaculately fresh palate with lovely fresh acids stretching out this wine's intense flavours to a lingering finish. Incredibly refreshing and zingy. A modern style that looks back to the past, translating the vineyard's instantly recognisable Marlborough-fresh flavours into a pure, highly focused and intense style. Sealed with a screwcap, but due to shortage of bottles mostly available only in cork this year.

Specialist wine stores, or Craggy Range Wines, phone (06) 877 7126, email: info@craggyrange.co.nz

★★★ **2002 Crossroads Hawke's Bay Destination**
$19-20 **Series Sauvignon Blanc**
Deliciously intense Hawke's Bay savvy that bears a strong resemblance to a really good, intense Marlborough sauvignon but has much softer, more approachable acids, making it hugely appealing.

Widely available.

★★½ **2001 Culemborg Sauvignon Blanc**
$10-11

This great-priced South African wine is zesty and fresh in flavour with hints of those tropical passionfruity tastes found in New Zealand savvies but with a lighter finish. Still, this is very good value for money.

🍷 *Liquor stores and supermarkets, or contact Federal Geo for stockists, phone (09) 578 1823, email: federalgeo@xtra.co.nz*

★★½ **2002 Dashwood Marlborough Sauvignon Blanc**
$16-18

Intense aromas of guava mix with classic Marlborough savvy smells like passionfruit and tropical fruit salad. This is a deliciously silky smooth wine, screwcapped and it benefits amazingly from this. Fantastically fruity and fresh and so guava-like it's almost hard to believe it's wine.

🍷 *Widely available.*

★★ **2002 Deakin Estate Sauvignon Blanc**
$12-13

This Australian sauvignon blanc is far more light-bodied than the majority of the full-flavoured and full-bodied savvies we are used to in New Zealand. It does have a recognisable gooseberry taste but tends to the lightish side in style and flavour.

🍷 *Widely available.*

★★½ **2002 Delegat's Marlborough Sauvignon Blanc**
$14-15

This big-name sauvignon blanc is also big on value in a medium-bodied style, erring on the light side but still fully Marlborough in flavour with gooseberries and fresh cut-grass aromas and tastes. Good value.

🍷 *Liquor King stores, Countdown, Foodtown, New World, Pak 'N Save, Woolworths.*

2002 Drylands Marlborough Sauvignon Blanc

★★ $18-19

Fresh grassy and slightly green-tasting sauvignon blanc from Marlborough. This wine is average value for money with a slightly tart finish.

🛒 *Widely available.*

2002 Esk Valley Hawke's Bay Sauvignon Blanc

★★★★ $19-20

It cannot just be because of the screwcap, but this gorgeously subtle wine is incredibly fresh in flavour. It is also a fresh take on New Zealand sauvignon blanc because of its lovely grainy texture in the mouth. It feels like a wine with guts and is well balanced with vibrant acids and a long finish.

🛒 *Widely available.*

2002 Forefathers Marlborough Sauvignon Blanc

★★½ $17-18

A lively, fresh, vibrant sauvignon blanc, which will woo instantly those who love the wow-factor in Marlborough savvies. Medium length and body. Reasonable value.

🛒 *Specialist wine stores, or contact Vintners New Zealand for stockists near you, phone (09) 979 2900, email: vintnersnz.co.nz*

2002 Framingham Marlborough Sauvignon Blanc

★★★ $19-20

For the first time this vintage, this wine is made with grapes from a new vineyard at Kaituna on the north bank of the Wairau River. It has fresh, intense passionfruity aromas and flavours with a bit of bite that Marlborough is known for. Deliciously sweet but finishes on a dryish note. Lovely quaffer with fish cooked in a sticky lemon Chinese sauce, or on its own.

🛒 *From Framingham, phone (03) 572 8884, email: framwine@voyager.co.nz*

★★½ **2002 Giesen Marlborough Sauvignon Blanc**
$16-17 A very herbal-tasting sauvignon blanc with kiwifruit and fresh cut-grass aromas and flavours. This is the sort of savvy that has harnessed a great following for New Zealand wines from overseas. It is lingering and zingy.

🍷 *Glengarry, North Island; First Glass and Fine Wine Delivery Company, Auckland; Moore Wilson, Wellington; or contact Burleigh Trading for more stockists, phone (09) 480 0789.*

★★★★ **2002 Gladstone Wairarapa Sauvignon Blanc**
$18-20 Here is one of the most deliciously rounded sauvignon blancs in the book this year. It comes from the ridiculously picturesque inland winery Gladstone, near Carterton in the Wairarapa. It tastes like fresh, ripe, sweet gooseberries with a dry finish.

🍷 *Gladstone Vineyard, phone (06) 379 8563.*

★★★ **2002 Goldridge Estate Premium Reserve Marlborough Sauvignon Blanc**
$18-19 Light, fresh sauvignon blanc fashioned in an easy-to-enjoy, drink-me-now style. It has deliciously zingy acids, stretching out the finish of the wine to a lingering gooseberry-tasting style.

🍷 *Foodtown supermarkets, specialist wine stores and liquor retailers.*

★★★★ **2002 Goldwater Dog Point Marlborough Sauvignon Blanc**
$19-20 Lively, bright and fresh sauvignon blanc with impressive length of flavour and a lovely smooth sweetish finish, sweet not at all in a cloying style but purely in terms of ripe, lovely, grapey flavours. Delicious! Sealed with a screwcap for the first time. I like the fact that the back label has a web address: www.goldwaterwine.com

🍷 *Specialist wine stores.*

★★★½ **2002 Greenhough Nelson Sauvignon Blanc**
$18-19 Like so many New Zealand wines, especially whites, this is sealed with a screwcap to keep it fresh and safe from cork taint, but also because screwcaps allow wine to taste exactly as it did when the winemaker finished it. This is an outstanding Nelson sauvignon blanc made by Andrew Greenhough. It has a focused, piercing acidity that is fantastically balanced by intense flavours that taste of pineapple, kiwifruit and guava – if your imagination is that fruity way inclined.

Specialist wine stores, or Greenhough Vineyard and Winery, phone (03) 542 3868.

★★★½ **2002 Grove Mill Marlborough Sauvignon Blanc**
$19-20 Very pale yellow-lemon colour with fantastic classic Marlborough gooseberry aromas and fresh bracing acids leading to a long finish, which is ripe and herb-edged at the same time, and also clean and fresh.

Most supermarkets and some specialist wine stores.

★★ **2002 Gunn Estate Sauvignon Blanc**
$14-16 Warm, fresh, tropical Hawke's Bay sauvignon blanc but a little light. Nice dry finish. Easy drinking but not special.

Widely available.

★★½ **Hardys Sauvignon Blanc**
$8-9 Young and fresh-tasting Australian sauvignon blanc with appealing sweet fruity flavours of light gooseberries and a zingy but soft acid finish. This is on the light side, but it's great value for money.

Widely available.

★★★ 2002 Hunter's Sauvignon Blanc Marlborough
$17-19

Pale-lemon colour with smooth texture and firm, zingy acids. When tasted the wine was very young but characteristically gooseberry-tasting with fresh grassy and ripe fruity flavours.

♛ Widely available.

★★★½ 2002 Johanneshof Cellars Marlborough Sauvignon Blanc
$18-19

Intensely tasty Marlborough sauvignon blanc with fresh, zingy, grassy flavours that remind you of summer with every whiff. Delicious stuff that is very well priced. Great value under $20.

♛ Specialist wine stores.

★★ 2002 Kaikoura Marlborough Sauvignon Blanc
$15-16

The grapes in this wine come from Marlborough but the name Kaikoura refers to the geographical region and name of the winery, just south of the Marlborough region. This is a slightly green-tasting white wine with a shortish finish. Average value for money.

♛ Specialist wine stores.

★★★ 2002 Kemblefield The Distinction Sauvignon Blanc
$19-20

Fresh and distinctive New Zealand style of savvy with flashes of gooseberry aromas and flavours. Its intense acids make it a good match with fresh panfried fish served with lemon.

♛ Wine Masters stores, Auckland; The Mill Liquorsave; Foodtown and Woolworths; or from the winery, phone (06) 874 9649, email: kew@kemblefield.co.nz

WHITE WINES

★★ **2002 Kemblefield Winemakers Signature**
$16-17 **Sauvignon Blanc**
Very light little brother of this winery's The Distinction Sauvignon Blanc. Fresh, hints of lemon in flavour and a medium finish.
 🍷 Point Wines and Cellar Select, Auckland; The Merchant of Taupo; Advintage, Hastings; Invercargill Licensing Trust; or from the winery, phone (06) 874 9649, email: kew@kemblefield.co.nz

★★★ **2002 Kim Crawford Marlborough**
$19-20 **Sauvignon Blanc**
Clean, fresh, zingy light white with lovely typical kiwifruit and gooseberry savvy characters and flavours.
 🍷 Glengarry, North Island; specialist wine stores nationwide.

★★½ **2002 Lake Chalice Marlborough**
$16-17 **Sauvignon Blanc**
Fresh, green, clean sauvignon with slightly green gingery finish. Slightly less than fully ripe but the flavour is fine in this herbal style.
 🍷 Glengarry and some other specialist wine stores, or Lake Chalice Wines, phone (03) 572 9327, email: wine@lakechalice.co.nz

★★ **2002 Lindemans Bin 95 Sauvignon Blanc**
$12-13 For New Zealanders who love sauvignon blanc, this is a tad disappointing. It is light in flavour and less intense than most savvies made on this side of the Tasman but subtler too, for those with a penchant for something simpler.
 🍷 Widely available.

★½ **2002 Longridge Hawke's Bay Sauvignon Blanc**
$14-15 Very light and simple sauvignon blanc with basic
flavours and slightly lacking fruitiness.
🛒 *Widely available.*

★★★ **2001 Maison Chandesais Sauvignon**
$14-15 **de Saint-Bris**
Refreshing French sauvignon blanc with savoury
flavours and a lovely lingering, grainy texture. Very
good value. If only it was more widely available! But
Chateauneuf does do mail order. Take advantage of it
and spread your wine wings.
🛒 *Chateauneuf store, 48 Pollen Street, Ponsonby, Auckland, or by mail order, phone (09) 378 7011, email: Chateauneuf@xtra.co.nz*

★★★ **2002 Matariki Stony Bay Sauvignon Blanc**
$16-17 Soft-textured sauvignon blanc with fresh and ripe
appley flavours. Easy to enjoy and good value.
🛒 *The Mill Liquorsave; Main Street Cellars, Waiuku; Birds Liquorsave, Thames; Corporate Direct, Wellington; and from Matariki Winery in Hawke's Bay, phone (06) 879 6226 or from the website: www.matarikiwines.co.nz*

★★★ **2002 Matua Hawke's Bay Sauvignon Blanc**
$14-15 This is fantastic tropical sauvignon blanc with floral and
fruit flavours of pineapple and apple and even a bit of
stonefruit nectarine taste to it. It is a little smoothie
with a soft, rounded body and decent finish. Great
value for the price too.
🛒 *Widely available.*

★★★½ **2002 Matua Matheson Sauvignon Blanc**
$17-18
For a top label this sports a bargain price. And it is also a smooth-textured, creamy little gem of a sauvignon blanc with all the bright fruit flavours you expect in good Kiwi savvies but a long, lingering, textural finish with a hint of savoury flavour tucked in. Fantastic wine.
Widely available.

★★★ **2002 Mills Reef Hawke's Bay Reserve Sauvignon Blanc**
$18-19
Has more weight and interest in both the flavour and the grainy, lingering texture, and is more of a New Zealand classic savvy than its little sibling above. Good value.
Widely available in supermarkets, wine stores nationwide, or contact Mills Reef Winery, phone (07) 576 8800.

★★½ **2002 Mills Reef Hawke's Bay Sauvignon Blanc**
$14-15
Light, fresh style without much concentration but clean and medium finish. Easy, clean quaffer. Reliable, not much more interesting than that.
Widely available in supermarkets, wine stores nationwide, or contact Mills Reef Winery, phone (07) 576 8800.

★★★ **2002 Mission Estate Marlborough/Hawke's Bay Sauvignon Blanc**
$14-16
This is a lovely intense-tasting wine with all the bells and whistles of classic good Marlborough savvy – fresh green-apple bite and a whiff of passionfruit aroma. Try it and see.
Widely available, or from Mission Estate Winery, phone (06) 844 2259.

★★★½ 2002 Montana Reserve Marlborough Vineyard Selection Sauvignon Blanc
$19-20

This Marlborough sauvignon blanc has hints of passionfruity appeal, and as the acids integrate more over the short-term it will get better. It has very good length of flavour and an appealing price tag too.

🍷 *Widely available.*

★★★ 2002 Montana Sauvignon Blanc
$14-15

Very classic Marlborough sauvignon blanc with fresh cut-grass flavours and aromas and a light to medium body. Good value early drinking style with a soft texture.

🍷 *Widely available.*

★★★ 2002 Mount Riley Marlborough Sauvignon Blanc
$15-16

Delivered by hand by Sheryle, who diligently ensures that wine writers get to taste the wine as well as those who buy this widely available, classically intense-tasting Marlborough sauvignon blanc. It has that piercing, refreshing acidity balanced nicely with ripe fresh gooseberry fruit flavours. Very clean and fresh and great value.

🍷 *Widely available.*

★★½ 2002 Ngatarawa Glazebrook Vineyard Selection Sauvignon Blanc
$17-18

It's obvious from the first whiff that this is a Kiwi sauvignon blanc but it is rounder and softer than most Marlborough savvies. That said, it still oozes fresh gooseberry flavours and kiwifruit notes.

🍷 *Restaurants and at the Ngatarawa Wines Cellar Door, Hawke's Bay, phone (06) 879 7603, email: ngatarawawines@clear.net.nz*

★★ **2001 Nobilo Fall Harvest Sauvignon Blanc**
$10-11 Very light but easy and soft sauvignon blanc with a touch of zing at the finish. Good with light, fresh panfried fish.
🛒 *Widely available.*

★★½ **2002 Nobilo Marlborough Sauvignon Blanc**
$11-12 This fresh gooseberry-tasting Marlborough savvy is exemplary value at this low price point. Zingy in aroma and vibrant in style without being over-the-top, it has a soft, smooth finish and is a good drink on its own.
🛒 *Widely available.*

★★ **2002 Okahu Estate Shipwreck Bay Sauvignon Blanc**
$14-16 There is less a hint of salty sea air about this wine and more of an inland vineyard in Te Kauwhata, which accounts for its lightly Kiwi gooseberry-tasting sauvignon blanc. This is soft in texture and easy to enjoy, in its light style.
🛒 *Specialist wine stores, or Okahu Estate Winery, phone (09) 408 0888.*

★★★ **2002 Pencarrow Martinborough Sauvignon Blanc**
$18-19 For a second-tier wine from New Zealand's most quality-focussed wine region, Martinborough, over the hill from the windy city, Wellington, this is deliciously zingy stuff. It has a green acid bite at the finish but lingers on a dry note. Delicious good-value quaffer.
🛒 *Specialist wine stores.*

★★½ 2002 Peregrine Central Otago Sauvignon Blanc
$19-20

Fresh Granny Smith apples and grassy-tasting deep-southern pinot noir made from one of the most picturesque wineries in Central Otago but with overtly high acids.

 Specialist wine stores, or at Peregrine winery, phone (03) 442 4000, email: peregrine@xtra.co.nz

★★½ 2001 Queen Adelaide Sauvignon Blanc
$9-10

This is great value, although light and simple in style. Australian sauvignon blanc often tastes less intense than many of the full-on New Zealand styles but this is clean and fruity – and good value for money.

 Widely available.

★★½ 2002 Riverside Wines Sauvignon Blanc
$12-14

This wine is made from grapes grown in the picturesque verdant land of the Dartmoor Valley, about 15 minutes' drive inland from Napier. It's an intensely aromatic Hawke's Bay sauvignon blanc with aromas of gooseberry and kiwifruit but light in flavour. Clean, light, well-made wine with an appealing price tag.

 Big Fresh, Foodtown, Woolworths, or from Riverside Wines, phone (06) 844 4942, email: riverside.wines@xtra.co.nz

★★ 2002 Robard & Butler Sauvignon Blanc
$10-11

Slightly dirty-smelling nose with nice fresh acids but a very light flavour.

 Widely available.

★★ **Ruben Hall East Coast Sauvignon Blanc**
$9-10 It tastes like sauvignon blanc but is buoyed up heavily by sweetness, which comes through on a slightly cloying finish. Average value only.
🧺 *Widely available.*

★★★½ **2002 Sacred Hill Marlborough Vineyards Sauvignon Blanc**
$14-16 Intense Marlborough zing, fresh and grassy, but modern dry finish. Lovely drinkable, refreshing style.
🧺 *Widely available.*

★★★ **2002 Sacred Hill Whitecliff Estate Sauvignon Blanc**
$14-16 Fantastic value, light, fresh Hawke's Bay sauvignon blanc, typically intense in a zingy New Zealand style with flavours of gooseberry and kiwifruit and also riper pineapple and tropical flavours. The finish is dry and the price tag surprisingly low, given the quality here. Buy heaps.
🧺 *Widely available.*

★★★ **2002 Saint Clair Marlborough Sauvignon Blanc**
$15-17 A very vibrant but slightly green-tasting Marlborough savvy which will woo those who love this pungent, full-on style. It has lovely zingy acids and very long, lingering flavours at the end of each mouthful. A great wine to eat with fresh panfried fish served with wedges of fresh lemon or lime.
🧺 *Widely available.*

★★½ **2002 St Helena Marlborough Sauvignon Blanc**
$14-16 Very light style of sauvignon blanc with freshness and hints of gooseberry flavours and a crisp acid finish. Would be good with spicy fish cakes.
🛒 *Widely available.*

★★½ **2002 Saints Vineyard Selection Marlborough**
$17-18 **Sauvignon Blanc**
Old-fashioned style with very green, herbaceous aromas and high acids and those full-on herby flavours of intensely distinctively Marlborough savvy.
🛒 *Widely available.*

★★½ **2002 Sanctuary Marlborough Sauvignon Blanc**
$14-15 Clean, fresh commercial sauvignon blanc with a light body and relatively sweet style giving it smoothness and early drinking appeal.
🛒 *Most supermarkets and some specialist wine stores.*

★★★½ **2002 Seifried Estate Sauvignon Blanc**
$18-19 Definitely a summer wine, this stunning number. It's sealed with a screwcap for the first time. Intense, zingy Nelson sauvignon blanc with overt green methoxyopyraxine flavours of herbs and freshly mown grass.
🛒 *Widely available.*

★★ **2002 Selaks Marlborough Sauvignon Blanc**
$14-15 A fresh New Zealand savvy with a slightly grassy green overtone and medium finish.
🛒 *Widely available.*

★★½ $15-16 — 2002 Shingle Peak Marlborough Sauvignon Blanc

This light white wine is part of the South Island range of Matua Valley wines, marketed under the evocative Shingle Peak label. It is a fresh but light sauvignon blanc and makes a good summer everyday wine.

🛒 *Widely available.*

★★½ $19-20 — 2001 Smithbrook Pembarton Sauvignon Blanc

Fresh, herby-tasting Australian sauvignon blanc with a light body and gooseberry flavours. Good length.

🛒 *Liquor King and specialist wine stores.*

★★★ $17-18 — 2002 Stoneleigh Marlborough Sauvignon Blanc

Fresh, grassy, typically Marlborough style with lovely flavours of fresh fruit; not as intense in flavour or smooth in texture as the Dashwood 2002 Marlborough savvy, but it's still very intense and great value.

🛒 *Widely available.*

★★½ $16-17 — 2002 Spy Valley Marlborough Sauvignon Blanc

A fresh, vibrant classic Marlborough sauvignon blanc with medium weight. Decent character and incredibly fresh and well made.

🛒 *Liquorland stores, Moore Wilson in Wellington, and other specialist stores. For more stockists, contact the winery, phone (03) 572 9840, email: j.estate@xtra.co.nz*

★★★ $16-18 — 2001 Stoneleigh Marlborough Sauvignon Blanc Rapaura Series

This intense-tasting, appley, kiwifruit- and gooseberry-flavoured sauvignon blanc has gorgeous texture in the mouth and great, long, zingy length.

🛒 *Widely available.*

★★ **2002 Stony Bay Sauvignon Blanc**
$14-16 Light-bodied, light-tasting sauvignon blanc with a slightly drying finish.
  🍷 *Specialist wine stores, or Matariki Wines, phone (06) 879 6226, email: wine@matariki.co.nz*

★★½ **2002 Tasman Bay Marlborough Sauvignon Blanc**
$15-16 This wine is made in Nelson with grapes grown just over the hill in Marlborough, the largest wine region in New Zealand. The wine is just a tad grassy in flavour with firm, unrelenting acids on the finish and a food-friendly, mouthwatering flavour that makes you long for fresh, simply panfried fish. Good value.
  🍷 *Widely available.*

★★★ **2002 Te Awa Farm Longlands Hawke's Bay Sauvignon Blanc**
$17-18 Very fresh, intense New Zealand sauvignon blanc from the country's second largest wine-producing region, Hawke's Bay. Its aromas and texture and flavours are all soft, and the acid structure throughout the wine is firm and strong from start to finish.
  🍷 *Specialist wine stores or contact the winery for more stockists, phone (06) 879 7602, email: winery@teawafarm.co.nz*

★½ **2002 Timara Sauvignon Blanc**
$9-10 A highly acidic sauvignon blanc buoyed up by sweetness and a shortish finish. Very basic white wine.
  🍷 *Widely available.*

★★★½ 2002 Trinity Hill Marlborough Sauvignon Blanc
$16-17
Winemakers John Hancock and Warren Gibson have fashioned the Marlborough grapes used in this wine to make a classic New Zealand sauvignon blanc in the typical Marlborough mould. It tastes of green Granny Smith apples and kiwifruit and lifted acids. Its zingy taste means it goes well with light, fresh fish.

🍷 *Widely available, or contact the winery, phone (06) 879 7778, www.trinityhillwines.com*

★★ 2002 Tuatara Bay Marlborough Sauvignon Blanc
$14-15
A second-tier wine from Saint Clair in Marlborough with a very green aroma and flavour from start to finish. Very average wine, which I suspect probably needed its grapes to have hung on their vines just a little longer than they did. Opt for this wine's big brothers, the always impressive Saint Clair sauvignon blancs.

🍷 *Saint Clair Estate Wines, phone (03) 578 8695, email: wine@saintclair.co.nz or www.saintclair.co.nz*

★★ 2002 Twin Islands Sauvignon Blanc
$15-16
Medium intensity of aromatics on this fresh, light young quaffing white. It has a hint of sweetness to balance the not-quite-ripe flashes of green flavour that shine through but offers okay quaffing.

🍷 *Big Fresh, Woolworths and specialist wine stores.*

★★½ 2002 Vidal Estate Hawke's Bay Sauvignon Blanc
$17-18
This is a soft but still-fresh style of sauvignon blanc with an attractive, slightly creamy texture and light, fresh medium style.

🍷 *Widely available.*

★★★½ **2002 Villa Maria Cellar Selection Marlborough**
$19-20 **Sauvignon Blanc**
Grapes from several different vineyards in Marlborough's Awatere and Wairau valleys go into making this fresh, bright sauvignon with an intense gooseberry taste and lingering finish.
🛒 *Widely available.*

★★★ **2002 Villa Maria Private Bin Marlborough**
$15-16 **Sauvignon Blanc**
This lively sauvignon blanc is made from Marlborough grapes by New Zealand's third largest winery, family-owned Villa Maria. It's fresh and clean with a touch of appealing sweetness at the finish.
🛒 *Widely available.*

★★★½ **2002 Waimea Estate Sauvignon**
$19-20
It's refreshing to taste such a good Nelson sauvignon blanc in flavour and style. This wine is incredibly similar to that intense, gooseberry-tasting Marlborough sauvignon style that put New Zealand on the world's wine map, but it is also a textural white with a long, lingering finish.
🛒 *Liquor King, Liquorland, most supermarkets.*

★★★★ **2002 Wither Hills Marlborough**
$19-20 **Sauvignon Blanc**
The screwcap seal of fresh, clean wine will soon be on all bottles of this brilliant-value sauvignon blanc. It has a lively, piercing acidity and lovely savoury flavours from the start. Five percent barrel fermentation adds texture that pushes up the savoury flavours.

🛒 *Countdown, Foodtown, Liquor King, Liquorland, New World, Super Value, Woolworths, some Super Liquor stores.*

★★½ **2002 Woollaston Estates Sauvignon Blanc**
$17-19 Fresh bright acids and clean lemon flavours are accentuated in this wine, especially those bottles sealed with a screwcap, which are more tamed and less obviously acidic than the wine when sealed under cork.

🍷 *Seriously Fine Wines and St Helier's Wines, or mail order from Woollaston Estates winery, phone (03) 542 3205, email: wine@WoollastonEstates.co.nz*

★★★ **2002 Woodthorpe Hawke's Bay Sauvignon Blanc**
$19-20
A lighter take on the New Zealand sauvignon blanc theme, driven more by its grainy texture than intense gooseberry or passionfruity flavours, as many expect from our sauvignons from this country.

🍷 *Specialist wine stores, or Te Mata Estate Winery, phone (06) 877 4399, email: wine@temata.hb.co.nz*

★★ **2002 Yalumba Oxford Landing Sauvignon Blanc**
$12-13 This Australian sauvignon blanc is typically lighter in aroma and flavour than its Kiwi counterparts and apart from the acid, which adds freshness, it is a tad lacking in character. It is clean and fresh and perfectly acceptable summertime drinking.

🍷 *New World, Pak 'N Save, specialist wine stores.*

SÉMILLON AND SÉMILLON-PREDOMINANT WHITE BLENDS

Sémillon is most famous for its role in sauternes, France's and the world's great dessert wine, in which sémillon is blended with sauvignon blanc and ages extremely well.

The best sémillon can age for decades, either as the best dry sémillons from Australia's Hunter Valley or as the best sweet ones from France, most notably of Chateau d'Yquem, prove.

In New Zealand sémillon is used predominantly as a blending grape with sauvignon blanc. Plantings of sémillon in this country have grown slowly over the last decade from 175 hectares nationwide in 1994 to 251 hectares in 2003, with predictions for a further 10 hectares to be planted over the next year. In tandem with this rise in the number of sémillon grapes grown in New Zealand, there is small growth in the number of stand-alone varietal sémillons being made in this country.

★★★ 2002 Babich Fume Vert Sémillon Chardonnay
$10-12

This is a surprisingly fresh, tasty white New Zealand blend of sémillon and chardonnay grapes. The sémillon adds the zesty lemon zing and the chardonnay gives it a bit of body. It's clean, honest, grapey-tasting wine and good value for money for everyday drinking.

Widely available.

★★ 2002 Banrock Station Sémillon Chardonnay
$9-10

Very simple Australian white wine made from sémillon and chardonnay grapes. Light and plain.

Widely available.

★★★ 2001 Beacon Hill Sémillon Chardonnay
$12-13

Light, creamy nuances with a hint of sweetness and a pleasing dry finish. A lovely clean, fresh simple quaffer, which is honest, pure dry white wine with tastes of both sémillon and chardonnay in every mouthful.

Specialist wine stores nationwide, or for more detail contact Lace Wines, phone (09) 828 4725.

★★★★ 2002 Glenguin The Old Broke Block Sémillon
$19-20

STAR BUY

Hunter Valley, dry-grown, low-yielding wine with a new, classier label. It's clean, limey and very stylish. New Zealand importer and Master of Wine Stephen Bennett is going to press this wine enthusiastically on restaurants. This wine is incredibly versatile with a wide range of foods.

Liquorland, Wine Masters and most specialist wine stores, or contact Bennett & Deller Wine Merchants, phone (09) 378 9463.

★★½ **2002 Jacob's Creek Sémillon Sauvignon Blanc**
$11-12 Don't be put off by the low price tag because this is great-value dry white with a hint of appealing sweetness in taste balanced by crisp acids.
🍷 *Widely available.*

★★★ **2001 Peter Lehmann Sémillon**
$15-16 Tarry charry nose with a dirty smell and light, lemon-fresh lanolin flavours. A good food wine with nice smooth texture and good length.
🍷 *Big Fresh, Foodtown, Woolworths and specialist wine stores.*

★★★ **2002 Rosemount Estate Sémillon Chardonnay**
$12-13 This Australian blend of sémillon and chardonnay is young but its flavours are a beautifully developed combination of lemony sémillon and a creamy-textured chardonnay. Together they work deliciously in this everyday white quaffer.
🍷 *Widely available.*

★★★ **2002 Trilogy Sémillon Sauvignon Blanc Viognier**
$15-16 Interesting combo of three grapes: the grassy lemony sémillon, which adds smoothness to the intensity of the sauvignon blanc, and the round, peachiness of the viognier. This is great value white wine from Australia with interesting flavours and textures.
🍷 *Specialist wine stores.*

★★★ **2001 Tyrrell's Wines Long Flat White**
$12-13 This iconic white wine is still around and still extremely popular. This vintage is a blend of both sémillon and sauvignon blanc grapes and makes a medium-bodied white with a hint of lemon flavour.
🍷 *Widely available.*

VIOGNIER

Viognier is a relatively sensitive grape variety, highly prone to wind and frosts, and therefore not at the top of the list for most winemakers who need more consistency than this grape usually offers. Consequently, very few viogniers are made in New Zealand, but those that are, ranging from light and green to peachy and rounded, all cost more than the $20 price restriction for this book.

Like those higher-priced wines, the viogniers featured here are surprisingly impressive dry white wines with a peachy perfumed aroma and taste and deliciously dry, spicy flavour.

Viognier's spiritual home is in the Rhône Valley in France, but in the last few decades it has also made inroads in Californian and Australian vineyards.

★★★ **2001 Georges Duboeuf**
$17-18
Great stuff, this French viognier. It's a lovely, lively, peachy, spicy wine with all the taste in the world, medium body and a style that is hard to define and easy to love. Great value too.
🛒 *Glengarry, North Island.*

★★★½ **2002 Les Salices Viognier Vin de Pays D'Oc**
$19-20
Here is a wine that tastes like wine rather than tropical fruit salad in a glass. It's fresh and spicy in a friendly, well-rounded style. Instantly likeable and great value – try this next time you feel like a chardonnay.
🛒 *Specialist wine stores, or contact Bennett & Deller Wine Merchants for stores near you, phone (09) 378 9463.*

★★★½ **2002 Yalumba South Australia Y Viognier**
$16-17

Quite delicious in a charming, peachy-bodied, easy-to-love sort of style. Big alcohol and not hugely definitive in style of fruit or flavour but pretty good value.
🛒 *Specialist wine stores.*

ROSÉ

Drink pink, says the tag line of the global campaign that relaunched Mateus Rosé last year. That particularly Portuguese pink wine might not go down in history as great, but it will bring new and young drinkers to the wine fold.

And like at least half of the rosés in this year's guide, it is fun not only in colour but also in flavour, with a freshness and softness that are hard to beat in simple everyday wines. Even better is that many of the rosés featured in this year's book, including many of the New Zealand wines as well as some of the French offerings, are better than any rosé previously available in this country. It seems that this wine style is finally being seen as a seriously fun wine that can and should taste as good as it looks.

Rosé is also known as blush, rosado (which the Spanish use for their light pink rosé) and clarete (used by the Spanish for darker-coloured rosé). Production of the famous Portuguese rosé, Mateus, was started at the end of World War II and peaked in the 1980s with over three million cases.

★★★ **2002 Ata Rangi Martinborough Summer Rosé**
$18-19
This wild berry-fruit-tasting rosé is made from cabernet sauvignon, which accounts for the slightly herbal edge, and pinot meunier, which adds zest and zing. It is one of New Zealand's best rosés purely because it is tasty enough to drink.

🍷 *Specialist wine stores, or Ata Rangi Wines, phone (06) 306 9570.*

★½ **Bertoulet Vin de Pays des Maures**
$10-11
Very light pink wine that lacks freshness.

🍷 *Chateauneuf store, 48 Pollen Street, Ponsonby, Auckland, or by mail order, phone (09) 378 7011, email: Chateauneuf@xtra.co.nz*

★½ **Côtes de Provence Mistral**
$9-10
This rosé is definitely a case of getting what you pay for. It's a plain-tasting, light-bodied pink with little fruit flavour to commend it.

🍷 *Chateauneuf store, 48 Pollen Street, Ponsonby, Auckland, or by mail order, phone (09) 378 7011, email: Chateauneuf@xtra.co.nz*

★½ **2000 Grain de Rosé**
$14-15
The most appealing thing about this wine is its tall, frosted bottle and beautifully quaint ornate gold label.

🍷 *Chateauneuf store, 48 Pollen Street, Ponsonby, Auckland, or by mail order, phone (09) 378 7011, email: Chateauneuf@xtra.co.nz*

★★ **2002 Hunter's Marlborough Rosé**
$14-15
I like the freshness and high acids that help counter the sweet fruity flavours here, but it lacks depth of fruit taste and body.

🍷 *Specialist wine stores, or Hunter's Wines, phone (03) 572 8489.*

★★ 2001 Isis Côtes du Marmandais
$12-13
This is the best-value under $15 rosé available from Chateauneuf store in Auckland. It's light and soft, but has a very short finish.

🍷 *Chateauneuf store, 48 Pollen Street, Ponsonby, Auckland, or by mail order, phone (09) 378 7011, email: Chateauneuf@xtra.co.nz*

★★★½ 2002 Kim Crawford Pansy
$17-18

STAR BUY

Like life, this wine is made to enjoy, says the back label. And it is an extremely enjoyable rosé sporting soft, sweet-cherry flavours. It is lightly fruity in taste but it's the clean fresh characters I like in this unmissable bottle sealed with its bright pink, unmissable screwcap. This is fantastic stuff!

🍷 *Kim Crawford Wine's cellar door only, Clifton Road, Te Awanga, Hawke's Bay, phone (06) 875 0553, www.kimcrawfordwines.co.nz*

★★★ 2001 Rivera Rosé
$16-17
Surprise yourself and buy some of this deliciously fresh, clean, strawberry-tasting Italian rosé. It is excellent value for money and made in a refreshingly modern style.

🍷 *Specialist wine stores, or contact importer Phil Clark at A Touch of Italy for more information, phone (09) 273 3701, email: sales@touchofitaly.co.nz*

★★★ 2000 Tavel Les Augieres
$17-18
This lively, bright red wine tastes deliciously zingy and fresh. It's soft and light, fresh and perfect for summer. Great value and stylistically poles apart from New Zealand rosé.

🍷 *Chateauneuf store, 48 Pollen Street, Ponsonby, Auckland, or by mail order, phone (09) 378 7011, email: Chateauneuf@xtra.co.nz*

★★½ **2001 Tavel Les Augieres**
$17-18
Lovely light, fresh, reddish-coloured rosé, just a tad hard on the finish but still a lovely pink summer drink with simple, light strawberry flavours.

🛒 *Chateauneuf store, 48 Pollen Street, Ponsonby, Auckland, or by mail order, phone (09) 378 7011, email: Chateauneuf@xtra.co.nz*

★★★½ **2002 Martinborough Vineyard Rosé** *(500ml)*
$15
This is the winery's second ever rosé from pinot noir and innovatively packaged in a 500ml bottle, which an 'older gentleman' recently described as the perfect-sized bottle 'for ladies who live alone'. Apparently he had the idea that such 'ladies' would start the bottle one night and finish it the next. The guy needs to get out more because there is no way this light and luscious strawberry-tasting rosé would last longer than half a night for most women. The 500ml bottle is a convenient size, though, and deliciously fresh.

🛒 *Specialist wine stores, or Martinborough Vineyard winery, phone (06) 306 9955.*

★★★ **Mateus Rosé**
$10-11
It won't surprise everyone to know that this is one of the cleanest, freshest rosés on the market. It's also one of the oldest, beginning its life in 1942 when Fernando Van Zeller Guedes founded Sogrape winery and created this wine, whose distinctive bottle is modelled on the flask bottles of World War I. It is very light but fresh and strawberry-like in taste. Good summer rosé, made from the Portuguese grape varieties baga, rufete, tinta barroca and touriga franca.

🛒 *Widely available.*

★★ **2002 Mills Reef Hawke's Bay Rosé**
$12-13
This Hawke's Bay rosé has a lovely intense, bright, deep-ruby colour but is very dull aromatically, and apart from being soft and creamy on the palate it has little flavour other than a discernible touch of sweetness.

🍷 *Widely available in supermarkets, wine stores nationwide, or contact Mills Reef Winery, phone (07) 576 8800.*

★★½ **2001 Nederburg Rosé**
$11-12
This South African rosé is light and refreshing when chilled, but a little short on fruit flavour and finish. Clean, simple rosé but just average value.

🍷 *Widely available.*

★★ **2002 Okahu Estate Shipwreck Bay Rosé**
$16-17
Smells slightly lollyish and tastes light and slightly insubstantial. Basic rosé, average value.

🍷 *Specialist wine stores, or Okahu Estate winery, phone (09) 408 0888.*

★★½ **2002 Sileni Cellar Selection Rosé**
$19-20
This lovely medium-coloured rosé is a little drying in texture and drier than most in style. Average value for money at this price, since it has flavour but is not overtly stylish or tasty wine. Very light in fruit flavour.

🍷 *Specialist wine stores, or Sileni Estates Vineyard and Winery, phone (06) 879 8768.*

★★★½ **2002 Unison Rosé**
$18-20
Anna-Barbara and Bruce Helliwell who make this refreshingly dry and refreshing dark pink rosé are purists in every sense, aiming for only top quality in all their winemaking. This is a fantastic example of that aim, a completely dry style. It seems, says Anna-Barbara, that rosé is underrated as a wine style in New Zealand, but they are convinced that with great grapes it can be a special and fresh summer wine style. This is a spicy, raspberry, strawberry-type fruit-salad-in-a-glass expression of that philosophy.

Unison Vineyard cellar door only, 2163 Highway 50, Hastings, phone (06) 879 7913.

BEAUJOLAIS AND GAMAY

It may seem surprising for New Zealand's only wine made from the same grape as beaujolais, gamay noir, to steal the limelight in this chapter but it was a clear winner. The wine is from Te Mata Estate's Woodthorpe Terraces in Hawke's Bay, and if it is any indication of what New Zealand winemakers can do with one of the world's earliest-ripening red grapes, then let's hope we see much more of it. The plantings of gamay noir in New Zealand are minuscule, especially when compared with its home in Beaujolais, France. The rest of the characteristically light reds in this chapter are good value for money, deliciously fresh and light but hugely drinkable.

There is, by the way, a world of difference in the quality and style of wines called beaujolais nouveau (produced fast for quick consumption) and beaujolais-villages wines, the best of which are often referred to, aptly, as poor man's pinot noir.

★★ **2000 Chateau Saint-Vincent Beaujolais-Villages**
$14-15   This wine still has that yeasty flavour of just-made reds that is often typical of beaujolais. It tastes light and cherry-like with a short finish.

🍷 *Chateauneuf store, 48 Pollen Street, Ponsonby, Auckland, or by mail order, phone (09) 378 7011, email: Chateauneuf@xtra.co.nz*

★★★ **2000 Domaine des Seigneurs Touraine**
$12-13   This is a warm, fresh, fruity beaujolais with a hint of sweet cinnamon and nutmeg spice. This is very good value for money.

🍷 *Chateauneuf store, 48 Pollen Street, Ponsonby, Auckland, or by mail order, phone (09) 378 7011, email: Chateauneuf@xtra.co.nz*

★★½ **2001 Georges Duboeuf Beaujolais-Villages**
$15-16   Very light, fresh beaujolais that has faded a little in flavour even one year down the track, but if you enjoy light reds in summer, it is good daytime drinking.

🍷 *Widely available.*

★★★ **2001 Joseph Drouhin Beaujolais-Villages Appellation Contrôlée**
$16-17   Lovely ripe cherry zing and it's only a villages wine. Has better body, more concentrated flavours and fresher fruit than a Waiheke Island pinot noir tasted alongside it. Lightish in colour with a smooth finish and medium length. Not a big serious beaujolais but deliciously drinkable with its soft tannins and smooth fruity finish.

🍷 *First Glass Wines and Wine Direct, Auckland; Regional Wines, Wellington; Vino Fino, Christchurch; Munslow's, Dunedin; or contact Wine Direct for more stockists, phone (09) 529 5267.*

★★½
$19-20
2001 Joseph Drouhin Julienas Appellation Controlée
More serious than the wine above from its first tarry, oaky whiff. Lovely soft tannins with a firmness that hints at a lot more life in this wine. Soft and sensuous fruit. A little cork-woody in aroma, but otherwise I like this wine.

🛒 First Glass Wines and Wine Direct, Auckland; Regional Wines, Wellington; Vino Fino, Christchurch; Munslow's, Dunedin; or contact Wine Direct for more stockists, freephone 0800 660 777.

★★½
$18-19
2000 Maison de la Dime Julienas
This is an appealing, juicy little red made from the gamay grape. It tastes like warm raspberries but is very light-bodied and has a shortish finish. Interesting, and easy to enjoy but a little steeply priced, especially given the quality of the New Zealand competition.

🛒 Chateauneuf store, 48 Pollen Street, Ponsonby, Auckland or by mail order, phone (09) 378 7011, email: Chateauneuf@xtra.co.nz

★★★½
$19-20

STAR BUY

2002 Woodthorpe Gamay Noir
What a fantastic expression of gamay grape this is! It's a lovely classic light red with soft fruit flavours and savoury, gamey qualities. Deliciously soft and smooth, and its soft tannins and relatively low acids make it so easy to drink and match with food. Brilliantly, surprisingly delicious.

🛒 Specialist wine stores, or contact Te Mata Estate Winery, phone (06) 877 4399, email: wine@temata.hb.co.nz

CABERNETS

CABERNET SAUVIGNON, CABERNET FRANC AND CABERNET-DOMINANT RED BLENDS

For winemakers, cabernet sauvignon is the red darling of the wine world. Relatively easy to transport, it is a late ripener but grows well in a wide range of soils, climates and countries. Cabernet sauvignon is a late-ripening grape, which makes it marginal for cool-climate growing conditions like New Zealand's South Island. It has thick skins, though, making it relatively resistant to rot, which is one of the biggest challenges to grape growers in New Zealand.

DNA fingerprinting has proven that cabernet sauvignon is a crossing of cabernet franc and sauvignon blanc.

It is more often than not blended with other grape varieties, most commonly with merlot, cabernet franc and malbec grapes. Although most of these wines are at the so-called budget end of the market, many have the ability to improve significantly with a little aging – some for up to five or more years.

★★★ 2000 Ashwood Grove Cabernet Petit Verdot Malbec
$15-16

Deliciously tasty Aussie red blend of cabernet sauvignon, petit verdot and malbec grapes, which all combine to make a flavour-packed red wine that tastes of sweet blackberries and wild raspberries and just a touch of mint. This is ripe all the way, delivering loads of value and taste for the price.

🛒 *Caro's, Point Wines and Fine Wine Delivery Company, Auckland; or contact Burleigh Trading for more stockists, phone (09) 480 0789.*

★★ 2000 Astica Cabernet Sauvignon
$11-12

A slightly simple red wine with a short finish and thin, fruity flavours.

🛒 *Wellsford Discount Liquor; Goldiggers, Thames; Pak 'N Save, South Island; or contact Burleigh Trading for more stockists, phone (09) 480 0789.*

★★★ 2001 Babich Hawke's Bay Cabernet Merlot
$18-20

This wine has lovely soft, sweet blackcurrant flavours with a beautifully rounded body, good balance and good length. Great value for money. What more could you want?

🛒 *Widely available.*

★★½ 2002 Banrock Station Cabernet Merlot
$14-15

Banrock Station is more than just a winery in an extremely warm part of Australia; it is a business that helps to take care of the endangered wetlands around the world. This wine is a light blend of cabernet sauvignon and merlot grapes, which together taste like blackberries and raspberries. Light, fresh, good value.

🛒 *Widely available.*

★★★ **2000 Bellingham Cabernet Sauvignon**
$17-18 This wine's fresh vibrant style and intensity of ripe fruit flavour show that sometimes you do get what you pay for. This is good-value red with sweet blackberry flavours and spicy anise characters. Flavoursome and medium-bodied.

🛒 *Liquor stores and supermarkets, or contact Federal Geo for stockists, phone (09) 578 1823, email: federalgeo@xtra.co.nz*

★★ **2000 Beresford Belleville Estate Cabernet Merlot**
$19-20 A light, minty-tasting Australian red blend of cabernet sauvignon and merlot. Pretty full on in its green minty flavours and just average value for money.

🛒 *Specialist wine stores nationwide, or for more detail contact Lace Wines, phone (09) 828 4725.*

★★½ **2000 Beresford St Aline Cabernet Shiraz**
$16-17 This is a very soft style of wine with hints of spice and licorice probably coming from the shiraz. Soft, quaffable style, a little hot and shortish on the finish but nice fleshy texture and flavour.

🛒 *Specialist wine stores nationwide, or for more detail contact Lace Wines, phone (09) 828 4725.*

★★★ **2000 Chateau de l'Abbaye Saint-Ferme**
$17-18 Smooth soft red from Bordeaux, France. This is not top-shelf Bordeaux but well-priced entry-level wine with classic blackberry flavours wrapped in a cedary flavour and light to medium body.

🛒 *Specialist wine stores, or contact Wine Direct for a store near you, or mail order, freephone 0800 660 777.*

★★½ **2000 Cheviot Bridge Cabernet Merlot**
$14-15 Here is another sweet Australian blend of cabernet sauvignon and merlot grapes. It tastes like warm, freshly made blackberry jam with a hint of spicy oak thrown in. A pretty one-dimensional red but will impress at a barbecue with its upfront flavours.
🍷 *Widely available.*

★★½ **2000 Clos Grangeotte Freylon Bordeaux Superiere**
$14-15 Very light French red from Bordeaux, the spiritual home of the cabernet sauvignon grape. This wine is a little lean in style with blackberry flavours but a short finish. Average value for money.
🍷 *Chateauneuf store, 48 Pollen Street, Ponsonby, Auckland; or by mail order, phone (09) 378 7011, email: Chateauneuf@xtra.co.nz*

★★ **2001 Collards New Zealand Cabernet Merlot**
$12-14 This is very light red with hints of green flavour and a slightly grippy finish. Okay for barbecue quaffing but otherwise opt for Collards merlot under the same label, which is warmer, more generous in flavour.
🍷 *Widely available, or from Collards winery, phone (09) 838 8341.*

★★★ **2000 Collards Rothesay Cabernet Sauvignon**
$16-18 Auckland winemaker Lionel Collard has always aimed to make wines that everybody wants to drink and that everybody can afford. He achieves the first part of that by sourcing grapes from all over New Zealand from which to produce wine at his West Auckland winery and the second part by being realistic. This is a lovely spicy red with medium body and length, made entirely from cabernet sauvignon grapes.
🍷 *Widely available, or from Collards winery, phone (09) 838 8341.*

★★★ 2001 Cookoothama Darlington Point Cabernet Merlot
$14-15

Good value quaffer for everyday drinking. This is an Australian red blend of cabernet sauvignon and merlot grapes, which tastes fresh and jammy and sweet.

🛒 *Specialist wine stores.*

★★½ 2001 Corbans Cabernet Sauvignon Merlot
$13-14

A very light-tasting red blend of cabernet sauvignon with merlot grapes. There is a firm tannin backbone underlaying the fruit flavours, but this wine is slightly out of balance. Average value.

🛒 *Widely available.*

★★ 2002 Corbans White Label Cabernet Sauvignon
$8-9

Very light cabernet sauvignon with an appealing price tag but relatively short, light flavours and finish.

🛒 *Widely available.*

★★½ 2002 Cottlers Bridge Cabernet Merlot
$9-10

Fresh blackberries with a hint of mint in this red. It's a bit sappy at the finish but easy to quaff and far better value, more robust, and with a longer finish than the straight 2001 merlot.

🛒 *Cellar Select and Wine Masters, Auckland; Advintage, Hastings. For South Island sales, contact Wine Masters, phone (09) 636 5240.*

★★½ 2000 Culemborg Cabernet Sauvignon
$12-13

Here is a light, fresh, great-value quaffing red from South Africa. It's an earthy, peppery-tasting cabernet sauvignon and good value at this price.

🛒 *Liquor stores and supermarkets, or contact Federal Geo for stockists, phone (09) 578 1823, email: federalgeo@xtra.co.nz*

★★★ **2000 De Bortoli Cabernet Merlot**
$17-18 Robust, clean, fruity Australian blend of cabernet, which adds backbone, and merlot, which gives soft sweet raspberry flavours. This is light in body and flavour but offers good value for money as a simple, consistently good red.
🛒 *Glengarry, North Island.*

★★½ **2001 Deakin Estate Cabernet Sauvignon**
$14-15 Fresh, sweet young cabernet sauvignon from Australia. This wine has a slightly grippy, drying finish, but the style is easy to enjoy, especially as a daytime drink, since it is fresh but light.
🛒 *Widely available.*

★★★ **2000 Deen De Bortoli Vat 9**
$14-15 **Cabernet Sauvignon**
This is a big, obvious Australian cabernet sauvignon with sweet jammy blackberry flavours at the start of each mouthful followed by lightly spiced oak at the end. The wine is great value for money for tasty everyday quaffing – buy a case for autumn and winter drinking.
🛒 *Glengarry, North Island; other specialist wine stores; or contact Marcus Pickens at Hancocks, phone (09) 379 3740.*

★★★ 2001 Delegat's Hawke's Bay/Gisborne Cabernet Merlot
$14-15

This red is a blend in more ways than one. Firstly, it includes grapes grown in both Hawke's Bay and Gisborne, and secondly, it is a classic mix of cabernet sauvignon with merlot, which combine here to make a slightly minty-tasting red with all the soft mid-palate of merlot with cabernet sauvignon's blackberry flavours and backbone.

Liquor King, Countdown, Foodtown, New World, Pak 'N Save, Woolworths.

★★½ 2000 Delegat's Reserve Cabernet Sauvignon
$19-20

Big blackberry flavours and lots of cedary-tasting oak impress from the first whiff of this medium-bodied New Zealand cabernet sauvignon. It is made with grapes grown in Hawke's Bay by one of the largest medium-sized wineries in the country.

Liquor King, Countdown, Foodtown, New World, Pak 'N Save, Woolworths.

★★★ 2000 Domaine d'Oustric Vin de Pays
$11-12

Fantastic value for money for a light cabernet sauvignon from France. This is fresh, sweet, appealing blackberries, and although the style is unashamedly light and the finish short, it's perfect for barbecues or when you just want to enjoy a glass of wine after work.

Chateauneuf store, 48 Pollen Street, Ponsonby, Auckland, or by mail order, phone (09) 378 7011, email: Chateauneuf@xtra.co.nz

★★★½ 2000 Domaine du Rochouard Bourgueil
$19-20
You can only buy this lively Christmas cake-tasting French cabernet franc at Chateauneuf. But it's worth beating a path to that French wine and food store in Auckland to be able to drink this sweetly spicy red wine, which is positively laden with cinnamon and dried-fruit flavours and has medium body.

Chateauneuf store, 48 Pollen Street, Ponsonby, Auckland, or by mail order, phone (09) 378 7011, email: Chateauneuf@xtra.co.nz

★★★ 2001 Eaglehawk Cabernet Sauvignon
$12-13
The word elegant best sums up this intense-tasting blackcurranty cabernet sauvignon from Australia. This is brilliant value for money and offers impressive flavour.

Widely available.

★★★½ 2000 Etchart Rio de Plata Cabernet Sauvignon
$11-12
This is proof that specialist wine stores offer fantastically good value for money, often in a far more tasty way than supermarkets do. This lovely Argentinian red tastes of blackberries and earthy spicy flavours. And if you can't find it, check out its siblings – Etchart merlot and Etchart malbec. All three are among the best-value wines in the book.

Specialist wine stores.

★★ 2000 Goldridge Estate Matakana Cabernet Merlot
$19-20
This is one of the few reds in this range made from grapes grown at the winery's region, Matakana, an hour's drive north of Auckland. The wine starts out as an elegant and restrained blend of cabernet sauvignon and merlot grapes but ends on a slightly herbal note.

Foodtown, specialist wine stores and liquor retailers.

★★★½ **1999 Gramps Cabernet Merlot**
$19-20
Great-value Australian red blend of cabernet sauvignon and merlot grapes from the famous Gramps winery in the sunny Barossa Valley. This is very tasty stuff, definitively fruity, and good with big flavours like juicy steaks and roasted beetroots or on its own.
🛒 *Specialist wine stores.*

★½ **Hardys Cabernet Sauvignon**
$8-9
This is a simple and light Australian red made with grapes grown in several different years, hence there is no vintage (single year) listed on the label. It's fresh and fruity but ends with a dry, slightly dusty taste.
🛒 *Widely available.*

★★★ **1999 Hardys Crest Cabernet Shiraz Merlot**
$14-15
This is one of the freshest, cleanest cabernet sauvignons in the book and very good value. It's oozing softness in texture and tannin and has a clean, blackberry flavour that lingers a little on the finish. It is balanced and tasty without being over-the-top in style.
🛒 *Widely available.*

★★★½ **1999 Hardys Insignia Cabernet Sauvignon**
$14-15
Fabulously good value, this Australian red. It is a pure and elegant expression of blackberry-tasting cabernet sauvignon but not so over-the-top in fruity, berry flavours that it leaves you stretching for a glass of water. This wine is refreshingly dry, spicy and clean.
🛒 *Supermarkets and liquor stores.*

★★½ **1997 Henry Lawson Mudgee**
$19-20 **Cabernet Sauvignon**
Lovely sweet-tasting, fruity cabernet sauvignon with light spicy flavours. A little drying at the finish.
Specialist wine stores.

★★★ **2000 Houghton Cabernet Shiraz Merlot**
$15-16 Fantastic-value red blend of the three grapes: cabernet, shiraz and merlot and made at the largest winery in West Australia. I like the honesty, elegance and pure fruit flavours of this wine, which is only slightly let down by a slightly short finish. It is outstanding value for money.
Widely available.

★★ **Jackman Ridge Cabernet Sauvignon**
$8-9 A non-vintage wine, meaning it is made with grapes grown in several different years rather than just one as is the norm. This is medium-dry in style with a short but lightly fruity finish. It's a bit tough in tannins but okay value for money.
Widely available.

★★★ **2000 Jacob's Creek Reserve**
$19-20 **Cabernet Sauvignon**
This deeply coloured Australian cabernet sauvignon tastes like blackcurrants and is stridently fruit driven. It's soft in texture and easy to enjoy, but the price is a little steep in relation to some of the other wines in this chapter.
Widely available.

★★★
$16-17
1999 Jamiesons Run Coonawarra Cabernet Shiraz Merlot
This southern Australian red has instantly appealing cocoa aromas and hints of chocolate and fruits with spiciness. Rich, plummy fruitiness. Medium finish. Reasonable length and depth.

🍷 *Widely available.*

★★½
$13-14
2001 JP Chenet Cabernet Syrah
This is exactly the light style of red wine that drinkers associate with merlot. It's a soft but pretty simple little number, reasonable value for everyday drinking when all you want is a little light fruity flavour in your wine.

🍷 *Liquor stores and supermarkets, or contact Federal Geo for stockists, phone (09) 578 1823, email: federalgeo@xtra.co.nz*

★★★
$16-17
2001 Kemblefield Cabernet Sauvignon Merlot Hawke's Bay
A clean, fresh, very soft, easy-to-enjoy blend of cabernet sauvignon with merlot grapes. The merlot gives the softness while the cabernet adds those instantly recognisable wild-berry flavours. It's pleasant drinking and very good value at this price.

🍷 *New Zealand Winemaker's Centre, Point Wines and Wine Masters, Auckland; Advintage, Hastings; Wakefields of Sumner, Christchurch; or from the winery, phone (06) 874 9649, email: kew@kemblefield.co.nz*

★★½
$15-16
2000 Kingston Cabernet Merlot
This Aussie red is a light, simple blend of cabernet sauvignon and merlot grapes. It's warm and fruity with a short finish. Average value.

🍷 *The Mill Liquorsave, Cellar Select, or contact Burleigh Trading for more stockists, phone (09) 480 0789.*

★★½ **2001 Kingston Cabernet Sauvignon**
$15-16 This is a ripe, blackberry-tasting red from Australia. It's good value for money but pretty one-dimensional in flavour and style.
🧺 *Contact Burleigh Trading for stockists, phone (09) 480 0789.*

★½ **2001 KWV Cabernet Sauvignon**
$16-17 This is a pretty thin South African red with a hint of greenness about the taste.
🧺 *Liquor stores and supermarkets, or contact Federal Geo for stockists, phone (09) 578 1823, email: federalgeo@xtra.co.nz*

★★★ **2000 La Consulta Finca la Celia**
$19-20 **Cabernet Sauvignon**
This Chilean cabernet sauvignon is easy to love with its savoury, earthy flavours and sweet, fresh thyme aromas and flavours. Good value for money too.
🧺 *Specialist wine stores.*

★★½ **2000 Le Cadet Cabernet Sauvignon**
$16-17 **Vin de Pays D'Oc**
A soft, smooth French red made under the 'country wine' status of Baron Philippe de Rothschild's lowest-tier label. This is a pleasant, easy-to-enjoy everyday red wine with light, fruity flavours and a clean finish.
🧺 *Glengarry, North Island; other specialist wine stores; or contact Marcus Pickens at Hancocks, phone (09) 379 3740.*

★★½ **2002 Lindemans Bin 45 Cabernet Sauvignon**
$12-13 Good-value sweet berry-tasting cabernet sauvignon with tasty cedary flavours and a lingering finish.
🧺 *Widely available.*

★★ **2001 Lindemans Cawarra Cabernet Merlot**
$9-10
Very light, fruity red with lots of spicy oak flavours lending this wine an attractive aroma but slightly drying finish. Average.
🛒 Widely available.

★★½ **1999 Lindemans Reserve Padthaway Cabernet Merlot**
$18-19
This wine is an impressively dark-red-coloured wine from South Australia. It tastes like sweet, ripe blackberry jam and is medium-bodied. All of that makes it good value for money, if you can forgive the slightly over-oaked style here.
🛒 Widely available.

★★½ **2000 Lindemans Reserve Padthaway Cabernet Sauvignon**
$18-19
A slightly over-the-top red from Australia that will find lots of keen red-wine fans out there. It is a little unbalanced, however, with its full-on taste of oak and slightly drying finish to all that intense blackberry-tasting fruit. A one-dimensional red.
🛒 Widely available.

★★ **2002 Lucknow Estate Cabernets Merlot**
$16-17
This Hawke's Bay red blend of cabernet grapes with merlot grapes lacks ripe flavours and ends on a short note. Average value for money.
🛒 New World in Lower Hutt and Wellington, and Lucknow Estate, phone (06) 874 9007, email: lucknow@xtra.co.nz

★★ **1999 Maglieri of McLaren Vale**
$18-20 **Cabernet Sauvignon**
At three years old, this Australian cabernet sauvignon is just a touch green in flavour and needs to be consumed soon. It has a medium body, but the blackberry tastes here are slightly smothered by a noticeable hint of greenness in flavour.
🛒 *Widely available.*

★★ **2001 Manara Rock Cabernet Sauvignon**
$14-15 This is a fresh new wine brand in New Zealand – it arrived on our shores in October 2002. This is a very light cab sauv with fresh, fruity flavours but a slightly grippy finish.
🛒 *Widely available.*

★★½ **2000 Matariki Stony Bay Cabernet Merlot**
$19-20 Ripe, sweet blackberry-tasting red that is very good value. This Hawke's Bay wine is a blend of cabernet sauvignon with merlot, grown by John and Rosemary O'Connor, both seasoned grape growers.
🛒 *The Mill Liquorsave; Main Street Cellars, Waiuku; Birds Liquorsave, Thames; Corporate Direct, Wellington; Matariki Wines, Hawke's Bay, phone (06) 879 6226 or from the website: www.matarikiwines.co.nz*

★½ **Mathew Lang Cabernet Sauvignon**
$8-9 Very light, simple Australian red with slightly fruity flavours but a short, slightly dirty finish.
🛒 *Widely available.*

CABERNETS

★★½
$16-17

2002 Matua Valley Hawke's Bay Cabernet Sauvignon Merlot

An average-value New Zealand red blend of the relatively late-ripening cabernet sauvignon grape with the earlier-ripening merlot. This wine is just a tad grippy at the finish, and although it boasts blackberry flavours in the mouth, it offers only average value for taste and price.

🍷 *Widely available.*

★★★½
$19-20

2001 Matua Valley Matheson Vineyard Hawke's Bay Cabernet Merlot

Ripe sweet fruit flavours combined with spicy, clean aromas make for elegant, top-tasting red that just sneaks into the price level for this guide.

🍷 *Widely available in supermarkets and wine stores, or phone (09) 411 8301, email: sales@matua.co.nz*

★★★
$11-12

2001 Matua Valley Settler Cabernet Sauvignon Shiraz

This is a fantastically soft, juicy sweet red with a dry finish but succulent mid-palate; so appealing and such fantastic value. Like Matua's Settler Chardonnay, this fabulous red blend is not only very affordable but fantastically tasty and drinkable. Buy it by the caseload.

🍷 *Widely available.*

★★½
$12-13

2000 Millstream Cabernet Merlot

This is very good, fantastic-value light South African red. It's a blend of cabernet sauvignon with merlot grapes and has a spicy finish. It's also definitely ready to drink up now, so go for it!

🍷 *Liquor stores and supermarkets, or contact Federal Geo for stockists, phone (09) 578 1823, email: federalgeo@xtra.co.nz*

★★ **2002 Mission Estate Hawke's Bay**
$14-16 **Cabernet Merlot**
A reasonable-value, average-quality red blend of cabernet and merlot from one of the country's oldest wineries, the Mission, in Hawke's Bay.

🧺 *Widely available, or from Mission Estate Winery, phone (06) 844 2259.*

★★ **2002 Mission Estate Hawke's Bay**
$14-16 **Cabernet Sauvignon**
This is a fresh young red for everyday drinking, with a hint of green flavour to it.

🧺 *Widely available, or from Mission Estate Winery, phone (06) 844 2259.*

★★½ **2001 Moculta Cabernet Merlot**
$19-20 It's easy to see why winemakers rave positively about the Barossa Valley in Australia; this is a warm, fruity red that seems to speak about its heat-filled origin in every tasty mouthful. My only gripe is that the finish is pretty short, but otherwise this is good value for money.

🧺 *Widely available.*

★★ **2001 Montana Cabernet Sauvignon Merlot**
$14-15 Here's a wine that is a case of 'read the small print'. It is a well-known New Zealand brand but made this year with grapes grown in Chile and New Zealand, which translates to a light young red with enough flavour for the dollars if all you want is a basic red quaffer for a quick after-work drink.

🧺 *Widely available.*

★★★½ 1998 Montes Reserve Cabernet Sauvignon Oak Aged
$19-20

This Chilean winery has forged a reputation for creating top-notch reds at the premium end of the market. This is a juicy, succulent cabernet sauvignon offering more interesting flavours than most of the wines in this chapter with its savoury, earthy tastes. Great value.

🛒 *Specialist wine stores.*

★★ 2002 Murray Ridge Cabernet Sauvignon
$9-10

Here's a case of getting what you pay for. This is basic quaffing at best, as its price tag suggests. Made from grapes grown in Australia, this is a simple red with sweet fresh-plum flavours and a slightly drying finish.

🛒 *Widely available.*

★★½ 2000 Nederburg Cabernet Sauvignon
$12-13

This is the cleanest, fruitiest and best value of the three Nederburg reds here, with more varietal purity than the other two cabernet sauvignon blends. It's sweet blackberries and sweaty, sweet leathery in flavour with a light finish but good value – especially with your favourite hearty barbecue food.

🛒 *Widely available.*

★½ 2000 Nederburg Cabernet Sauvignon Merlot
$12-13

A slightly dusty-tasting South African red blend of cabernet sauvignon and merlot. Low price tag, short finish, slightly below average value.

🛒 *Widely available.*

★★   **1999 Nederburg Cabernet Shiraz**
$12-13

Simple fruity South African red that is a little dried out on the finish, which is short. If you have it, drink up now; otherwise wait till the next, fresher vintage comes along.

🛒 *Widely available.*

★★★   **2000 Nobilo Fall Harvest Cabernet Shiraz**
$10-12

This New Zealand-branded wine is made with grapes grown in Australia. The blend of cabernet sauvignon and shiraz grapes in this wine makes a deliciously soft, spicy and fruit-driven wine. This is fantastic value for money and so easy to drink as a light summer red or a warm-up winter wine after work.

🛒 *Widely available.*

★½   **2000 Nottage Hill Cabernet Shiraz**
$11-12

A light, green-tasting Australian red blend of cabernet and shiraz. This is a multi-vintage wine, hence no one year is listed on the label.

🛒 *Widely available.*

★★½   **2002 Odyssey Kumeu Cabernet Sauvignon**
$14-16

This is a light-tasting red made from grapes grown in Kumeu, West Auckland. Its flavours run the gamut from sweet blackcurrants to a hint of mint, but it has a noticeably green taste at the end of each mouthful. Well made but average value.

🛒 *Specialist wine stores.*

★★★ 2001 Penfolds Koonunga Hill Cabernet Merlot
$17-18

Showing some nice aged development characters, although the tannins are pretty hard in this wine. The fruit is lovely but it is covered in tannins that are woody and dry on the tongue and at the end of each mouthful. This is a disappointing character in this wine. I like the clean, earthy characters on the nose.

🛒 *Widely available.*

★★½ 2002 Penfolds Rawsons Retreat Cabernet Sauvignon
$13-14

This is great value every year with appealing sweet berry flavours in the middle of every mouthful and a round, soft texture. Good buying.

🛒 *Widely available.*

★★★ 2001 Penfolds Thomas Hyland Cabernet Sauvignon
$19-20

Mint and eucalypt aromas and flavours run through this wine, which is surprisingly elegant in style, with sweet blackberry and blackcurrant intensity in the middle of each mouthful. Good price, great value.

🛒 *Widely available.*

★★★ 2000 Preece Cabernet Sauvignon
$17-18

Gutsy Aussie cabernet sauvignon with minty flavours and aromas leading into a luscious, surprisingly juicy, blackberry-tasting cabernet sauvignon. Clean, fresh and vibrant in a definitely Australian style.

🛒 *Liquor King and specialist wine stores.*

★★★ 2002 Queen Adelaide Cabernet Sauvignon
$9-10
This is one of the best-value cabernet sauvignons in the book and one of the softest in flavour and tannins. All of which means buy it by the half case for basic everyday glass-after-work wine. Sweet, juicy berry flavours are accompanied with light smoky oak aromas.
🛒 *Widely available.*

★★½ 2000 Redbank King Valley Cabernet Merlot
$19-20
A very young, minty-tasting red that is a little grippy on the finish, made from grapes grown in one of Australia's coolest wine-growing climates, in the King Valley north of Melbourne.
🛒 *Specialist wine stores.*

★★★★ 1999 Richmond Grove Coonawarra Limited Release Cabernet Sauvignon
$19-20

Buy a case of this sensational red! It's made only from cabernet sauvignon and tastes intensely blackberry-like, with a gamey hint softening out that full-on fruitiness. Fantastic value and it is developing deliciously in the bottle, showing it would be a good prospect for cellaring for a few years.
🛒 *Specialist wine stores.*

★★ 2000 Riverside Wines Dartmoor Cabernet Merlot
$14-16
Like the straight merlot in the Riverside wine stable, this red tastes a little green, but I like its cabernet backbone, which adds weight to the wine, filling out the middle palate. Average value for money.
🛒 *Big Fresh, Foodtown, Woolworths, or from Riverside Wines, phone (06) 844 4942, email: riverside.wines@xtra.co.nz*

★★★ **2002 Robard & Butler Cabernet Sauvignon**
$10-11
This wine is lighter in style but so much better balanced than its sibling blended with merlot, featured below. I especially like the sweet lightness of blackcurrant flavours tucked into the subtle spicy wrapping around this red. Great value.
Widely available.

★★½ **2002 Robard & Butler Cabernet Sauvignon Merlot**
$10-11
Hugely appealing because of its intense hit of dark, sweet blackberry flavours, which are supported by an underlay of spicy, cedary oak that tastes slightly drying at the finish. Good buying for everyday quaffing wine.
Widely available.

★★★ **2001 Robert's Rock Cabernet Sauvignon Merlot**
$12-13
Savoury, earthy flavours combine in this wine with a sweet chocolatey-tasting red.
Liquor stores, or contact Federal Geo for stockists, phone (09) 578 1823, email: federalgeo@xtra.co.nz

★★★ **2002 Rosemount Estate Cabernet Merlot**
$12-13
The stylish purple diamond label on this bottle conceals a soft red blend of cabernet sauvignon with merlot grapes. Its tannins are soft and smooth. The style is fruity but light and easy to enjoy after work in summer. Very good value.
Widely available.

★★★½ 2000 Rosemount Estate Cabernet Sauvignon
$15-16
This robust Australian red tastes young and fresh, even at nearly three years old. It is blackberry- and raspberry-tasting but still needs time, and if you are looking for something to cellar, check this one out. Buy half a case and taste it every six months to enjoy its evolution in style.
🧺 *Widely available.*

★½ Ruben Hall Cabernet Sauvignon Merlot
$9-10
This is a very light, greenish blend of cabernet sauvignon with merlot grapes. A bit simplistic and basic with a grippy finish.
🧺 *Widely available.*

★★★ 1998 Russet Ridge Cabernet
$19-20
Big, fruity, full-on Australian red with impressively intense blackberry and boysenberry flavours and spicy oak adding extra body. Lovers of big bold reds will find this wine irresistible.
🧺 *Specialist wine stores.*

★★★½ 2001 Sacred Hill Whitecliff Vineyards Merlot
$14-16
Sweet, fresh, light, lovely flavours in a relatively robust style with heaps of mid-palate weight and flavour. What great value for a cheapie New Zealand merlot! Shows what the right clones and good viticulture can do. Fantastic value.
🧺 *Widely available.*

★★½ **2001 Saints Cabernet Sauvignon Merlot**
$16-17

This cabernet sauvignon offers a lot more generosity than many New Zealand cab merlot blends in this price range, with some sweet blackberry-styled warm fruit flavour and spicy notes adding interesting complexity. The finish is a little short, but otherwise it's good stuff and good value.

🛒 *Widely available.*

★★★ **2000 Salena Estate Cabernet Sauvignon**
$16-17

Australian cabernet with fresh, intense blackberry flavours and a slightly short finish but good value for money at this price; team it up with a juicy steak and you'll be wowed by the wine's ability to work well with meaty flavours and still shine through.

🛒 *Specialist wine stores, or contact Vintners New Zealand for stockists near you, phone (09) 979 2700, email: vintnersnz.co.nz*

★★½ **1999 Seifried Estate Cabernet Merlot**
$19-20

Hermann Seifried made this wine with grapes grown in Nelson, which is relatively cool for this style of wine – the cabernet component of the wine tastes a tad leafy green, which is nicely rounded out by the softness of the merlot's round body and its sweet fruit style. Good everyday quaffer at the upper end of the price spectrum in this context.

🛒 *Widely available.*

★★ **2001 Selaks Cabernet Sauvignon**
$14-15

A slightly green-tasting, light-bodied New Zealand red.

🛒 *Widely available.*

★★★ **2001 Silky Oak Cabernet Merlot**
$12-13
This is a very light red blend of cabernet sauvignon and merlot and, like the other two wines in this range, it's a well-made, well-balanced wine, making it great value for money.

🍷 *Liquor stores and supermarkets, or contact Federal Geo for stockists, phone (09) 578 1823, email: federalgeo@xtra.co.nz*

★★★ **1999 Sir James Cabernet Shiraz Merlot**
$18-19
The regal-sounding Sir James label has always had a fantastic bubbly in its range, and this red blend of cabernet sauvignon and shiraz with merlot grapes is also excellent value. It's warm and fruit driven from the moment you take your first whiff, opening into a juicy, sweet plummy-tasting red and then finishing with a light, warm taste of raspberries.

🍷 *Liquorland.*

★★★ **2000 Stepping Stone Cabernet Sauvignon**
$14-15
Sweet ripe-fruit flavours in this wine made with grapes grown on the Limestone Coast in South Australia and part of the Stonehaven range of wines. That sweet blackberry thing really kicks in here all the way from the first whiff to the last mouth-taste at the finish. Its tannins are a little coarse on the finish, but this is a ripe-tasting wine in the classic South Australian mode of eucalypty-type flavours, though not nearly so overt as the merlot. Definitely the better of the two, with a longer, softer and smoother finish. Good value for money.

🍷 *Widely available.*

★★ 2001 Stony Bay Cabernet Merlot
$18-20

Average-value New Zealand red blend of cabernet sauvignon and merlot with minty overtones and a clean, fresh style.

🛒 Specialist wine stores, or Matariki Wines, phone (06) 879 6226, email: wine@matarikiwines.co.nz

★★★½ 2001 Tatachilla Breakneck Creek Cabernet Sauvignon
$14-15

Very affordable sweet-tasting Australian cabernet sauvignon. Good everyday drinking or for barbecue quaffing in summer. This is a medium-bodied red.

🛒 Foodtown, New World, Woolworths, specialist wine stores.

★★★★ 2001 Tatachilla Partners Cabernet Shiraz
$14-15

This Australian blend of cabernet sauvignon and shiraz grapes is fantastic value for money, providing huge satisfaction with its gorgeous ripe blackberry fruit and loganberry flavours and spicy finish.

🛒 Foodtown, New World, Woolworths, specialist wine stores.

★★★½ 2001 Taylors Estate Cabernet Sauvignon
$18-19

A surprisingly weighty Australian cabernet sauvignon with freshness, medium body and even a touch of lingering fruit at the slightly drying finish. This is elegant cabernet sauvignon at a good price.

🛒 Widely available.

★★★ 2000 35 South Cabernet Sauvignon
$16-17

Tasty Chilean cabernet sauvignon with delicious, tasty earthy and savoury flavours in a clean, multi-layered package of flavour.

🛒 Specialist wine stores.

★★★½ 2001 Thorn Clarke Sandpiper Cabernet Sauvignon
$18-20

The Barossa Valley in Australia is better known for producing great grapes for shiraz, but this impressively tasty cabernet sauvignon is also made with grapes grown there. I like its sweet, rich flavours and lingering finish, and it is extremely good value for money.

Huapai Wines & Spirits and Rosedale Liquor, Auckland; Munslow's, Dunedin; or contact Burleigh Trading for more stockists, phone (09) 480 0789.

★★½ 2001 Timara Cabernet Sauvignon Merlot
$9-10

This easily affordable red is fresher than many wines costing a third more. It has soft, sweet berry flavours and an overt oaky taste and texture, which leaves the finish a tad short but otherwise it's an easy-to-enjoy, good-value everyday wine.

Widely available.

★★½ 2001 Trapiche Estate Cabernet Sauvignon
$14-15

This Argentinian cabernet sauvignon is light bodied with hints of earthy flavour and a clean style. It tastes of light, fresh blackberries and spice.

Southern Liquor, Blenheim; Super Liquor and Regional Wines, Wellington; or contact Burleigh Trading for more stockists, phone (09) 480 0789.

★★★½ 1999 Trapiche Oak Cask Cabernet Sauvignon
$18-19

What great value this wine is! Its staunch oak backbone leads into a succulent and juicy-tasting Argentinian cabernet sauvignon with very good lingering flavours.

Wine Masters and Cellar Select, Auckland; Regional Wines, Wellington; Woolworths; or contact Burleigh Trading for more stockists, phone (09) 480 0789.

★★★½ 2000 Trilogy Cabernet Sauvignon Cabernet Franc Merlot
$15-16

Deliciously good value with big black colour and perfumed aromas of spicy cloves and intense blackcurrants. This is a lovely soft wine, too, from the addition of merlot in the blend, which tends to have softer tannins than cabernets.

🛒 *Specialist wine stores.*

★★★ 2001 Trinity Hill Shepherds Croft Hawke's Bay Merlot Cabernets Syrah
$18-19

Fresh raspberries and a soft texture make this zingy little red instantly appealing. Good value and very concentrated and ripe in flavour for this price.

🛒 *Widely available or contact the winery, phone (06) 879 7778, www.trinityhillwines.com*

★★ 2001 Twin Islands Cabernet Sauvignon Merlot
$18-19

A slight hint of green on the nose and in the palate, which reminds me of a green capsicum flavour. Average value.

🛒 *Big Fresh, Woolworths, specialist wine stores.*

★★ 2001 Tyrrell's Long Flat Vineyard Red Cabernet Sauvignon Shiraz Malbec
$12-13

An earthy-tasting Australian red blend of three grapes, including the well-known cabernet sauvignon and shiraz and the lesser-known malbec, which adds colour and sweetness to the wine's flavour. Basic quaffing.

🛒 *Widely available.*

★★½ **2001 Tyrrell's Old Winery Cabernet Merlot**
$15-16
Big, bold Australian red blend of cabernet sauvignon and merlot grapes, with a hint of minty flavour at the end of each mouthful. Average value for money for this ever-so-popular style of red.
Widely available.

★★ **2001 Tyrrell's Wines Moore's Creek Cabernet Sauvignon**
$13-14
Very simple, light-bodied and overly sweet Australian red made from cabernet sauvignon.
Glengarry, North Island.

★★ **2001 Villa Maria New Zealand Private Bin Merlot Cabernet Sauvignon**
$16-17
This wine is made with grapes grown on the East Coast of New Zealand and, although very light, it's a step up in quality from the cabernet sauvignon-merlot blend above because of its purity of flavour and fresh plum tastes.
Widely available.

★½ **Villa Maria New Zealand Vintage Cabernet Sauvignon Merlot**
$16-17
Look beyond the big black letters saying 'New Zealand' to the small print, which says this wine is made with grapes grown in Chile, New Zealand and Australia. This is a light style of red with a slightly drying finish.
Widely available.

★★★½ 2000 Villa Montes Cabernet Sauvignon
$14-15

A great-tasting Chilean cab sauv with backbone, oomph and flavour to burn. Think gutsy, earthy flavours and rich, sweet licorice and blackberries, all intermingled in a stylish fashion. Great value. Buy heaps.

🍷 *Glengarry, North Island; or contact Marcus Pickens at Hancocks for more information, phone (09) 379 3740.*

★★★½ 2001 Wally's Hut Cabernet Merlot
$11-12

Nobody's saying who Wally is but this is one exceptional blend of cabernet sauvignon and merlot grapes, grown in south Australia. Adjectives like intense, balanced, beautifully tasty and lingering spring to mind after a single sip of this lovely red. Buy a case of it and enjoy over the next couple of years.

🍷 *Glengarry, North Island; or contact Marcus Pickens at Hancocks for more information, phone (09) 379 3740.*

★★½ 2001 Wally's Hut Cabernet Shiraz
$11-12

Warm, fresh and tasty, this is a more gutsy, obvious style of red than its softer, subtler sibling above. Still good value for money for a lightly fruity everyday red to sip after work.

🍷 *Glengarry, North Island; or contact Marcus Pickens at Hancocks for more information, phone (09) 379 3740.*

★★½ 2000 Windy Peak Victoria Cabernet Shiraz Merlot
$17-18

A slightly simple red blend of three grapes: cabernet sauvignon, shiraz and merlot. This Australian red has jammy sweet flavours and a drying finish and is average value for money.

🍷 *Glengarry, North Island; or contact Marcus Pickens at Hancocks for more information, phone (09) 379 3740.*

★★½ **2000 Wolf Blass Cabernet Merlot**
$18-19
This is a pretty minty-tasting red wine with sweet fruit flavours but a short finish.

🛒 *Glengarry, North Island; or contact Marcus Pickens at Hancocks for more information, phone (09) 379 3740.*

★★★ **1999 Wolf Blass South Australia Cabernet Merlot**
$18-19
Lovely ripe-tasting wine with rich aromas and flavours of spice, hints of aniseed, sweet plums and a touch of integrated oak flavours. Very easy-to-drink wine in which the only detracting factor is a slightly drying textural taste at the finish. Otherwise this is good value for money.

🛒 *Widely available.*

★★★ **2000 Wolf Blass South Australia Cabernet Sauvignon Yellow Label**
$18-19
Medium-bodied Australian cabernet sauvignon with some complexity in its flavour profile, offering savoury, cedary tastes as well as that cabernet's typical blackberry fruit flavours.

🛒 *Widely available.*

★★★½ **2000 Wyndham Estate Bin 444 Cabernet Sauvignon**
$14-15
This is an incredibly consistent Australian cabernet sauvignon, one of that country's best reds each year if value for money is what you judge wine by. Buy half a case to enjoy in winter.

🛒 *Widely available.*

★★★ 2000 Wyndham Estate Bin 888 Cabernet Merlot
$14-15

Blackberry flavours and soft textures combine in this Australian blend of cabernet sauvignon and merlot. It's good value at this price for a reliably easy-to-enjoy red in a light style.

Widely available.

★★½ 2001 Wyndham Estate Cabernet Shiraz Ruby Cabernet
$9-10

This Australian red is a blend of three grapes, including cabernet sauvignon, shiraz and ruby cabernet. It's very light and fruity with a soft texture and appealing price tag. My only complaint is that it has a slightly short finish.

Widely available.

★★★½ 1999 Yalumba Barossa Cabernet Shiraz
$19-20

An impressively staunch blend of cabernet sauvignon and shiraz grapes, all of which were grown in the Barossa Valley. The cabernet seems like a little bit of a tough nut to crack, but the shiraz adds a plummy sweetness.

Specialist wine stores.

★★ 2001 Yalumba Oxford Landing Cabernet Shiraz
$12-13

Light, fresh and simple quaffing red that is a bit thin on fruit richness and flavour, but for this price it offers acceptable daily quaffing, if you're not expecting to delve deeply into thought about the wine.

New World, Pak 'N Save, specialist wine stores.

CÔTES-DU-RHÔNE

The words 'Côtes-du-Rhône' have become synonymous with the taste of light, spicy red wine, vaguely fruity at best and sometimes a little coarse. Wines bearing the name Côtes-du-Rhône Villages are usually a significant step up in quality from their basic Côtes-du-Rhône counterparts, largely because maximum yields per grapevine for the latter are far less, resulting in wines that taste more concentrated in flavour.

All of these wines come from France's Rhône Valley, which is divided into four regions.

★★★ **2000 Caves de Rasteau Côtes-du-Rhône**
$16-17 This is deliciously good value for money because it has more body and flavour than most Côtes-du-Rhône. Although gutsy in style, it is soft in texture and plummy in flavour.

🛒 *Chateauneuf store, 48 Pollen Street, Ponsonby, Auckland, or by mail order, phone (09) 378 7011, email: Chateauneuf@xtra.co.nz*

★★½ **2000 Delas Côtes-du-Rhône St Esprit**
$19-20 Light, fruity and fresh with a hardish finish but only average value at this price. Still, I like its earthy and clean characteristics.

🛒 *Foodtown, New World, Woolworths, specialist wine stores.*

★★★ **1999 Domaine Capouilleres Côtes du Ventoux**
$12-13 Easy-to-love French red with a fantastically affordable price tag. The flavours here are a tasty mélange of savoury, peppery and plummy tastes. Soft in texture and great value.

🛒 *Chateauneuf store, 48 Pollen Street, Ponsonby, Auckland, or by mail order, phone (09) 378 7011, email: Chateauneuf@xtra.co.nz*

★★★½ **1999 Les Classes Côtes-du-Rhône Villages**
$14-15 This is the best Côtes-du-Rhône in the book, and it's exceptionally good value at under $15. Fruity and spicy in a Christmas cake type of style, it is luscious, clean and vibrant with medium length. The sort of wine you can drink heaps of before you realise the bottle is empty.

🛒 *Chateauneuf store, 48 Pollen Street, Ponsonby, Auckland, or by mail order, phone (09) 378 7011, email: Chateauneuf@xtra.co.nz*

★★ **1999 Paul Jaboulet Aine Les Traverses**
$15-16 **Côtes-du-Rhône**
Very light and simple red from France. This is light-bodied and light-flavoured with hints of earthiness but a short finish.
🍇 *Specialist wine stores.*

★★★ **2000 Paul Jaboulet Aine Parallele '45'**
$19-20 This is the tastier and better value by far of the two Paul Jaboulet wines in this chapter. It's syrah as we know and love it: peppery, savoury, clean and spicy, with a fleshy plum taste and soft finish. Good value for money too.
🍇 *Specialist wine stores.*

★★★ **2000 Santa Duc Selections Les Blovac Rasteau**
$19-20 Light-bodied, savoury-tasting red wine with spicy, peppery flavours overlying fresh fruitiness.
🍇 *Specialist wine stores, or contact Wine Direct for a store near you, or for mail order, freephone 0800 660 777.*

GRENACHE

Grenache is the world's second most planted grape variety and is particularly prolific in south France and in Spain, where it is known as garnacha. Although grenache is best known in this part of the world as a relatively light style of red wine, it is also one of the grapes used to produce some of the world's great French reds, Chateauneuf-du-Pape.

Until the 1960s, grenache was Australia's most planted red grape variety. A little grenache is grown in New Zealand, but it is generally considered to need a slightly hotter climate than this country can boast. Time will tell.

Grenache blanc is the white grape form of grenache noir.

★★★½ **2001 D'Arenberg Stump Jump Grenache Shiraz**
$14-15
This lovely sweet, fruity blend tastes more like a shiraz than a grenache, although there is that lovely spicy underlay of grenache on which shiraz lays its head. Fantastic value for money and fabulous tasting too.
🍷 *Specialist wine stores.*

★★ **1998 Domaine de le Cypriere Vacqueryas**
$19-20
This grenache from southern France is very light on fruit flavour with a heady aroma of earthiness. It's a little dirty in style and flavour but will fit in well with meaty barbecue food.
🍷 *Chateauneuf store, 48 Pollen Street, Ponsonby, Auckland, or by mail order, phone (09) 378 7011, email: Chateauneuf@xtra.co.nz*

★★★½ **2000 Domaine Saint-Pierre Corbières**
$15-16

STAR BUY

Another fantastic grenache from France's once highly respected Corbières region. This is so tasty it is almost unbelievable that it costs only around $16. Flavours run the gamut of black plum, white pepper and aniseed to an indefinable earthy but clean finish. Great value.
🍷 *Chateauneuf store, 48 Pollen Street, Ponsonby, Auckland, or by mail order, phone (09) 378 7011, email: Chateauneuf@xtra.co.nz*

★★★½ **1998 Gramps Grenache**
$19-20
This is incredibly smooth, soft, tasty grenache with surprising oomph. Its flavours are rich, sweet black cherries, but beware, the 14 percent alcohol still sneaks up on you after a glass or two of this tasty little number. It only just creeps into the price level but offers so much flavour that it is great value for money.
🍷 *Specialist wine stores.*

★★½ 2001 Jacob's Creek Grenache Shiraz
$11-12 Reliably good-value light-bodied quaffing blend of grenache and shiraz. Not mind-blowing but surprisingly consistent in taste and style from year to year. Good buying.

Widely available.

★★★½ 2000 Lesquerde Côtes du Roussillon Villages
$14-15 This stunning little beauty from the south of France is pure grenache and boasts an impressive intensity of flavour for just $15. It is sweet, warm and instantly appealing, with clean, fruity flavours of wild berries and a hint of earthiness about it. Great value for money.

Chateauneuf store, 48 Pollen Street, Ponsonby, Auckland, or by mail order, phone (09) 378 7011, email: Chateauneuf@xtra.co.nz

★★★ 1999 Moculta Barossa Valley Grenache
$15-16 This is an intensely sweet grenache that will remind some drinkers more of shiraz with its dark colour and almost plummy sweet flavours. It is warmer and lighter in taste than shiraz, easier as a quick-drinking red and, since its tannins are very light, this could also be very tasty on a hot day served slightly chilled.

Widely available.

★★ 2001 Peter Lehmann Grenache
$15-16 Light cherry flavours wrapped in a thin, cardboardy texture. A bit dirty and thin and a bit rough in texture, which is a shame given its lovely sweet light potential.

Big Fresh, Foodtown, Woolworths, specialist wine stores.

★★★ 1998 Prieure du Chateau de Segure Fitou
$17-18

Wow! This gutsy French take on grenache will blow all your expectations of this grape, which tends to be light and cherry-like. This is a flavour-packed version with hints of black pepper and a light body but moreish finish. Great value for money.

🛒 *Chateauneuf store, 48 Pollen Street, Ponsonby, Auckland, or by mail order, phone (09) 378 7011, email: Chateauneuf@xtra.co.nz*

★★★ 2001 Rosemount Estate Grenache Shiraz
$12-13

Attractive, warm and fruity everyday drinking red from Australia. This wine is made from a blend of grenache and shiraz grapes, which are light and fresh. It's a simple, easy-to-enjoy style with a short, slightly drying finish but plenty of warmth to add appeal.

🛒 *Widely available.*

★★½ 2000 Synergy Grenache Shiraz
$18-19

A fresh, slightly herbal-tasting light red from Australia. Just average value here.

🛒 *Contact Burleigh Trading for stockists, phone (09) 480 0789.*

★★★½ 1999 Yalumba Barossa Bush Vine Grenache
$19-20

This evocatively named grenache is made from grapes grown on low bush vines, which help give it a fresh flavour of sweet, dark redcurrant taste. It is relatively robust and medium-bodied. Very good wine under $20 and great value for money.

🛒 *Specialist wine stores.*

MALBEC

Malbec is the most planted grape variety in Argentina and the Cahors region in south-west France.

Malbec has traditionally been used as a blending grape in cabernet sauvignon-based wines, so it has been hidden in the mix rather than seen on the label. Now it is increasingly being used as a stand-alone grape variety to make wine labelled 'malbec', and some of the world's most promising examples are produced in Argentina.

Very little malbec is grown in New Zealand, but plantings have increased substantially in the last decade from just nine hectares in 1991 to 145 hectares this year.

Malbec is also known as pressac and cot.

★★★ 2000 Angaro Finca La Celia Malbec/Syrah
$14-16

Lovely Argentinian blend of the gutsy, deeply coloured malbec grape with the softer, more sensuous syrah, which adds a smooth and zingy fresh black-plum flavour and texture to this wine. This is an unusual combination of grapes that work well together, providing a wine that is very good value for money.

🍷 *Specialist wine stores, or contact Wineworks Solutions, phone (09) 816 8494.*

★★★ 2001 La Consulta Finca la Celia Malbec
$19-20

This is a gutsy-tasting, purple-coloured Chilean malbec, full of big, ripe, sweet flavours in an obviously wintery style. Good value for those who like their wines big and bold.

🍷 *Specialist wine stores, or contact Wineworks Solutions, phone (09) 816 8494.*

★★★½ 2000 Montes Reserve Malbec Oak Aged
$19-20

STAR BUY

This Chilean red is an iron fist in a velvet glove. It's packed with flavour and has a fruity tannin structure, and it is so fabulously soft and sweet that it is velvet-smooth in feel. Flavourwise, it has everything from sweet mixed berries to hints of aniseed. Fantastic value for money.

🍷 *Specialist wine stores.*

★★★½ 2001 Rio De Plata Malbec
$11-12

Ignore the country's politics because this fantastic-value Argentinian red is part of a new wave of outstandingly good wines from that country. It's gutsy, soft, sweet, meaty, nicely balanced and a great price. This sort of value is hard to beat.

🍷 *Specialist wine stores.*

★★½ **2000 Trapiche Estate Malbec**
$14-15
This is an interesting Argentinian red with body and oomph and light fleshy flavours of plums and spice. It is good value but the best malbec in the book is this wine's big sibling, below.
🛒 *The Mill Liquorsave, Super Liquor, Woolworths, or contact Burleigh Trading for more stockists, phone (09) 480 0789.*

★★★½ **1999 Trapiche Oak Cask Malbec**
$18-19
This is Argentinian red at its best. This lovely bright, fleshy-tasting red wine has medium body and rich fruitcake flavours. It finishes on a clean, lingering and spicy note. Great value for money.
🛒 *Wine Masters, Auckland; Liquorette, Northcote; Regional Wines, Wellington; or contact Burleigh Trading for more stockists, phone (09) 480 0789.*

MERLOT AND MERLOT-DOMINANT REDS

In the minds of most cabernet-lovers, merlot plays second fiddle to the often-stauncher cabernet sauvignon. But merlot on its own makes one of the world's top wines in the form of Petrus from Bordeaux, not to mention a host of other wines considered at least as good, also from Bordeaux and increasingly from other countries and regions like California in the United States, Victoria in Australia, Hawke's Bay in New Zealand, and also various valleys in Chile.

As a blending partner with cabernet sauvignon, merlot often fills in the gaps with softness and sweet, fruity appeal.

It ripens earlier than cabernet sauvignon, making it easier to grow in relatively cool grape-growing climates like New Zealand.

★★½ 2000 Ashwood Grove Merlot
$15-16

This is a very light-tasting Australian merlot without the oomph that good merlot can have but with the recognisable warm fruitiness that merlot-lovers enjoy. A good wine for beginners and better than average value.

🍷 *Villa Winery, Auckland; Rosedale Liquor, Albany; New World Centre City, Wellington; some South Island supermarkets; or contact Burleigh Trading for more stockists, phone (09) 480 0789.*

★★ 2001 Astica Merlot Malbec
$11-12

This Argentinian blend of merlot and malbec grapes is the second-tier wine from the large Trapiche winery. This is a light, relatively sweet style of red with a short, drying finish. Good for beginners.

🍷 *Pak 'N Save, South Island; or contact Burleigh Trading for more stockists, phone (09) 480 0789.*

★★★ 2000 Baron Philippe de Rothschild Le Cadet Merlot Vin de Pays D'Oc
$16-17

Bright red in colour with lovely sweet fresh fruit but a very short finish which is a little astringent in texture. A good quaffer, though, with lovely savoury characters.

🍷 *Glengarry, North Island; other specialist wine stores; or contact Marcus Pickens at Hancocks, phone (09) 379 3740.*

★★★½ 2000 Brajkovich Kumeu River Merlot
$14-15

Sealed with a screwcap for the first time and undoubtedly much fresher for it. Warm, fresh merlot berry flavours, a tad green on nose but impeccably made merlot on the palate. Has soft tannins, rich raspberry flavours with gorgeous clean freshness and surprisingly good length for a wine this price. Great quaffing, good value.

🍷 *Widely available, contact Kumeu River Wines for stockists, phone (09) 412 8415.*

★★½ 2000 Collards Hawke's Bay Merlot
$19-20

Very light, fresh red with all that softness wine drinkers have come to expect from merlots made for everyday drinking and a hint of spice to add some kick to the length.

🍷 *Widely available, or from Collards winery, phone (09) 838 8341.*

★★★ 2002 Coopers Creek Hawke's Bay Merlot
$16-17

Light berries and minty aromas on the nose lead into lovely mocha chocolate flavours on the palate. Nice, easy quaffing red at a very appealing price.

🍷 *Foodtown supermarkets and most wine stores.*

★★ 2001 Cottlers Bridge Merlot
$9-10

A greenish-tasting red with minty flavours and a sappy, astringent finish. Not special.

🍷 *Cellar Select and Wine Masters, Auckland; Advintage, Hastings. For South Island sales, contact Wine Masters, phone (09) 636 5240.*

★★½ **2001 Crossroads Destination Series**
$19-20 **Merlot Cabernet**
This is a relatively light red wine with easy-to-enjoy sweetish fruit flavours like raspberries and a slightly dry but tasty spicy finish. It offers interesting flavour but only average value at this price.

🛒 *Liquor stores and supermarkets, or contact Federal Geo for stockists, phone (09) 578 1823, email: federalgeo@xtra.co.nz*

★★ **2000 Culemborg Merlot**
$12-13 This South African wine is an earthy, savoury-tasting wine that is slightly astringent, drying merlot, lacking warmth of fruit flavour.

🛒 *Liquor stores and supermarkets, or contact Federal Geo for stockists, phone (09) 578 1823, email: federalgeo@xtra.co.nz*

★★ **2001 Deakin Estate Merlot**
$13-14 Basic everyday drinking merlot which offers very light fruit flavours and a short finish. Good for a quick after-work drink or at a barbecue.

🛒 *Widely available.*

★★½ **2001 Delegat's Reserve Merlot**
$19-20 This dark-coloured merlot is made with grapes grown in Hawke's Bay and rich in fleshy, sweet plummy flavours. It has a hint of mint about its taste but has enough body and flavour to impress mid-week dinner guests.

🛒 *Liquor King, Countdown, Foodtown, New World, Pak 'N Save, Woolworths.*

★★★ 2002 Drylands Marlborough Merlot
$18-19

Very fresh, sweet raspberry-tasting merlot from ripe, flavoursome Marlborough-grown grapes, with a hint of spice at the finish. Dry and great value for money.
🛒 *Widely available.*

★★ 2001 Eaglehawk Merlot
$12-13

This is light, fresh and fruity but lacks warmth and length. Okay as a barbecue or basic party wine.
🛒 *Widely available.*

★★★ 2000 Equinox Hawke's Bay Merlot Cabernet Sauvignon
$19-20

Shows loads of promise for merlot at this price, which is more robust and riper and more complex when grown in Hawke's Bay. This is a spicy, chocolatey-tasting wine with plummy flavours and juicy texture. Delicious.
🛒 *Equinox Wines, email: sales@equinoxwines.co.nz*

★★★½ 2001 Gladstone Wairarapa Merlot Cabernet Sauvignon
$18-20

This Wairarapa red is a real surprise – soft, sweet, juicy and luscious in both taste and texture. It's silky and smooth and impressively, explosively plummy-tasting. Great value for money, so buy lots.
🛒 *Specialist wine stores, or from Gladstone Vineyard, phone (06) 379 8563.*

★★ 2000 Goldridge Estate Hawke's Bay Merlot
$19-20

Drying, astringent red from Hawke's Bay with medium fruit flavours but lacking character and warmth.
🛒 *Specialist wine stores and liquor retailers.*

★★½ **2002 Gunn Estate Merlot Cabernet**
$14-15
This blend of merlot and cabernet sauvignon grapes, both grown in the Bay, is a light-to-medium-bodied red with fresh berry flavours and a tangy acid finish. Average value at this price.
Specialist wine stores.

★★½ **2001 Hanging Rock Merlot**
$15-16
Cool packaging, hot wine. There is major fruit flavour in this little Victorian merlot, which tastes of sweet black grape juice. It is short on the finish but so tasty and easy to enjoy that this represents good value for money.
Glengarry, North Island; other specialist wine stores nationwide.

★★ **2001 Hardys Varietal Range Merlot**
$8-9
This warm, sweet merlot tastes like light blackberries wrapped in a soft, lightly spicy oak flavour. It is a one-dimensional red with simple flavours but an attractive price tag.
Widely available.

★★ **2000 Huntaway Reserve Merlot Cabernet Sauvignon**
$19-20
Very light with fresh raspberry flavour but pretty thin.
Liquor stores and specialist wine stores.

★★★ $18-20

2001 Hunter's Marlborough Merlot Pinot Cabernet

The pinot is of course pinot noir and the blend is a bit unusual for New Zealand, but I like the creamy texture and soft sweet flavours; it reminds me of a Kiwi version of a fleurie or Brouilly Beaujolais; those fruit-driven styles where the tannins are still quite robust. This unusual blend works deliciously well. Serve it chilled with spicy food.

Specialist wine stores, or contact Hunter's Wines, phone (03) 572 8489.

★★ $8-9

Jackman Ridge Merlot

A non-vintage wine, meaning it is made from a blend of grapes grown in different years. As many merlots in this price range are, this one tastes all soft and light with fresh berry flavours. Good value under $10.

Widely available.

★★½ $11-12

2001 Jacob's Creek Merlot

A teeny bit of a step up from the wine above, this one has fresher, sweeter, more concentrated flavours, but it is a relatively light-bodied and light-flavoured merlot with fresh raspberry tastes and a short finish. Not bad value.

Widely available.

★★★ $16-17

2000 Jamiesons Run Coonawarra Merlot

Sweet, plummy merlot from Coonawarra, not so green as the cab shiraz-merlot blend. Quite a yummy wine with soft sweet flavours at the start although a little hollow in the mid-palate.

Widely available.

★★ 2002 Kim Crawford East Coast Merlot
$19-20

Slightly minty in aroma and flavour, made with grapes grown on the east coast of the North Island. Average value for money.

Glengarry, North Island; specialist wine stores nationwide.

★★ 2001 Kingston Merlot
$15-16

Light, fresh but slightly green-tasting merlot with a hint of mint and a short finish. Very average value for money.

Advintage, Hastings; Point Wines, Auckland; or contact Burleigh Trading for more stockists, phone (09) 480 0789.

★★½ 2001 KWV Merlot
$16-17

This is a very light South African merlot with a hint of raspberry flavour mid-palate and a slightly grippy finish. Pretty average value for money at this price.

Liquor stores and supermarkets, or contact Federal Geo for stockists, phone (09) 578 1823, email: federalgeo@xtra.co.nz

★★ 2002 Lake Chalice Merlot
$18-20

A light, bright, slightly green-tasting merlot in the old Marlborough mould, with creamy nuances supposed to soften this out, but a sappy finish lets it down.

Glengarry, some other specialist wine stores, or Lake Chalice Wines, phone (03) 572 9327, email: wine@lakechalice.co.nz

★★★½ **2001 Les Salices Merlot Vin de Pays D'Oc**
$17-18

It's defined as country wine by the words 'vin de pays' and it is from one of the most adventurous regions in France's highly regulated wine industry. This is lovely rich-flavoured merlot with juicy, sweet red plum and cherry flavours and soft, ripe fruit tannins. This is a steal. Buy loads.

🍷 *Specialist wine stores, or contact Bennett & Deller Wine Merchants for stores near you, phone (09) 378 9463.*

★★ **2002 Lincoln Winemakers Series Gisborne Merlot**
$19-20

Basic red wine made with grapes grown in Gisborne. This one has more oomph than many merlots in this chapter but it tastes light and green. Very average.

🍷 *Liquorland and Cellar Select, or contact Lincoln Vineyards, phone (09) 838 6944, email: wine@lincolnwines.co.nz*

★★ **2002 Lindemans Bin 40 Merlot**
$12-13

A light, fresh Australian merlot with flavours of blueberries and raspberries and a slightly short finish. This is a one-dimensional wine and average value for money.

🍷 *Widely available.*

★★½ **2001 Lindemans Cawarra Merlot**
$9-10

This is a surprisingly sweet and juicy Australian merlot with a great-value price tag.

🍷 *Widely available.*

★★½ **2000 Lindemans Reserve Padthaway Merlot**
$18-19 Instantly attractive red with intense and concentrated flavours of blackcurrants but a slightly drying oaky finish, which arrests the warmth of the fruit flavour.
🛒 Widely available.

★★½ **2001 Longridge Merlot Cabernet Sauvignon**
$14-15 This red blend of merlot with cabernet sauvignon is very light in fruit flavour but has a hint of fruity warmth at the front of the palate. Simple and short.
🛒 Widely available.

★★★ **2001 Ca Montini Luna di Luna Merlot Cabernet**
$18-19 The vibrant red bottle contains a deliciously flavoursome and soft Italian red blend of merlot and cabernet sauvignon grapes. Surprisingly good, given the gimmicky bottle. Savoury, lingering and light. Good value for money too.
🛒 Specialist wine stores, or contact importer Phil Clark at A Touch of Italy for more information, phone (09) 273 3701, email: sales@touchofitaly.co.nz

★★½ **2000 McPherson's Merlot**
$13-14 Warm, sweet fruity Australian merlot that has a great price tag, generous sweetness at the beginning of each sip and slightly short finish. Good value for everyday drinking.
🛒 Liquor stores and supermarkets, or contact Federal Geo for stockists, phone (09) 578 1823, email: federalgeo@xtra.co.nz

★★½ **2002 Matua Hawke's Bay Merlot**
$16-17
Pretty lean merlot with some sweet fruitiness about it but not a lot of body or generosity of style. Average value for money at this price.
🍷 *Widely available.*

★★★ **2001 Michel Laroche Merlot**
$16-17
Light, fresh red from the south of France. Good value for money with its sweet fruitiness and hint of minty flavour.
🍷 *Specialist wine stores.*

★★ **2001 Mills Reef Hawke's Bay Merlot Cabernet**
$16-17
A bit light and green, grippy at the finish. Unripe fruit tannins kick in at the end.
🍷 *Widely available in supermarkets, wine stores nationwide, or contact Mills Reef Winery, phone (07) 576 8800.*

★★★ **2002 Mission Estate Hawke's Bay Merlot**
$14-16
Warm, fresh, fruity young red, which is great value for money and a lovely interpretation of the new wave of New Zealand merlot.
🍷 *Widely available, or from Mission Estate Winery, phone (06) 844 2259.*

★★★ **2001 Montana Reserve Barrique Matured Merlot**
$19-20
This is a tasty New Zealand merlot made by the country's largest winery, Montana Wines. In flavour it tastes predominantly spicy with hints of fleshy fruit and dark plummy overtones. The finish is medium.
🍷 *Widely available.*

★★★½ **2000 Montes Reserve Merlot**
$19-20 A fantastic red wine from Chile's Colchagua Valley. This wine towers above most of the other merlots in this chapter with its deliciously concentrated berry flavours, which are as intense as they are tasty. There is an earthy finish but it's clean and sweet at the same time. Great value for money.
♛ *Specialist wine stores.*

★★½ **2002 Murray Ridge Merlot**
$9-10 Very light red wine with soft, sweet berry flavours but a short finish. This is good value for a couple of basic after-work glasses of plonk.
♛ *Widely available.*

★★ **2000 Nobilo Fall Harvest Merlot**
$10-12 A light red made with grapes grown in France. This is fresh and berry-like in taste with a slightly metallic finish.
♛ *Widely available.*

★★ **2001 Nottage Hill Merlot**
$11-12 This wine's very sweet blackcurrant flavours end on a slightly drying, short note. Pretty average stuff.
♛ *Widely available.*

★★½ **2001 Okahu Estate Shipwreck Bay**
$16-17 **Merlot Chambourcin Pinotage**
This red blend of merlot, Chambourcin and pinotage tastes lightly cherryish and soft but is short in flavour and average value for money.
♛ *Specialist wine stores, or Okahu Estate Winery, phone (09) 408 0888.*

★★½ 2000 Preece Merlot
$17-18 A light, berry-tasting merlot with a smooth mid-palate but slightly drying finish. Average value.
🍷 *Liquor King and specialist wine stores.*

★½ 2001 Queen Adelaide Merlot
$9-10 This is a very light red with little fruit flavour to commend it.
🍷 *Widely available.*

★★★½ 2001 Rio De Plata Merlot
$11-12 Like the malbec in this Argentinian range of wines, this is fantastic value for money. It's far more gutsy than most of the merlots in this chapter and offers incredibly good value for money with its bright, shiny, earthy and satisfying red-plum flavours. Buy a case before it zooms off store shelves.
🍷 *Specialist wine stores.*

★★ 2001 Riverside Wines Dartmoor Merlot
$14-16 A very light, old-fashioned and green-tasting merlot, slightly sour, made from Hawke's Bay grapes grown in the Dartmoor Valley.
🍷 *Big Fresh, Foodtown, Woolworths, or from Riverside Wines, phone (06) 844 4942, email: riverside.wines@xtra.co.nz*

★★½ 1999 Rosemount Estate Merlot
$15-16 Warm, instantly appealing, friendly Australian merlot. This wine has relatively light berryfruit flavours supported by a backbone of tannic oak, adding body and weight to the wine. Very drinkable in a big, bold sort of way.
🍷 *Widely available.*

★★★½ 2002 Sacred Hill Whitecliff Estate Hawke's Bay Merlot
$15-16

It's not just the price of this wine that makes it amazing value. The taste is all sweet fruity berries from start to finish. It is a blend of mainly merlot with a small addition of malbec, cabernet franc and cabernet sauvignon grapes blended into this intensely sweet-tasting, medium-bodied wine. It has a lingering finish and is great value for money.

Widely available, or from Sacred Hill Wines, phone (06) 879 8760, email: enquiries@sacredhill.com

★★½ 2001 Saint Clair Marlborough Merlot
$19-20

Merlot made its mark with wines like this soft, fresh, fleshy, fruity red. It's light and spicy but slightly grippy at the finish. Perfectly good daytime quaffing and provides exactly the merlot experience most wine drinkers expect.

Widely available.

★★★ 2002 Silky Oak Merlot
$12-13

This is one of the best merlots under $15 with its sweet fruit flavour and robust, spicy characters. Great value for money, offering more flavour than most merlots at this price.

Liquor stores and supermarkets, or contact Federal Geo for stockists, phone (09) 578 1823, email: federalgeo@xtra.co.nz

2001 Spy Valley Marlborough Merlot
★★★ $19-20

Like all the new Spy Valley wines, this one is fab stuff, especially for a red from Marlborough. Winemaker Alan McCorkindale was brought in to make this vibrant red Marlborough merlot, which has fleshy red plummy tastes and a creamy finish. Stylish stuff.

🛒 *Glengarry, some other specialist wine stores, or Lake Chalice Wines, phone (030 572 9327, email: wine@lakechalice.co.nz*

2000 Stepping Stone Merlot
★★½ $14-15

A Stonehaven wine (made from grapes grown on the Limestone Coast in South Australia), sporting overt eucalypt flavours on the nose, which carry through in the mouth in an instantly recognisable, quintessentially Australian fashion. This wine is a good quaffer in a slightly less than ripe style but with soft, juicy fruit textures. Slightly short finish.

🛒 *Widely available.*

2001 Tatachilla Breakneck Merlot
★★★ $14-15

Sweetly appealing Australian merlot with warm berry flavours welcoming the wine drinker on to sip after sip. Good value for money.

🛒 *Foodtown, New World, Woolworths, specialist wine stores.*

2001 Taylors Estate Clare Valley Merlot
★★★ $18-19

Lovely juicy, sweet merlot with ripe, rich fruity flavours of incredibly sweet raspberries with a spicy, slightly short finish. Good value drinking.

🛒 *Widely available.*

★★½ **2002 Timara Oak Aged Merlot**
$9-10
A light, fresh red with clean, plummy flavours but an astringent woody finish. It's far better value for money than the white but still a bit tough in texture.
🧺 Widely available.

★★★ **2001 Wyndham Estate Bin 999 Merlot**
$14-15
Very light, spicy merlot with hints of raspberry flavours wrapped in a soft outer. This is where merlot begins to be good value. Light and simple but easy to enjoy.
🧺 Widely available.

★★ **2001 Yalumba Oxford Landing Merlot**
$12-13
This is a very light, basic, big-brand red made from merlot. Soft, but simple.
🧺 New World, Pak 'N Save, specialist wine stores.

★★★ **2000 Yalumba Y Merlot**
$15-16
A stylish new label added to the Yalumba range last year fills a mid-tier gap in quality with this wine, offering far more than its little siblings. For only a few dollars more you can get rich fruitcake spice and tannic backbone in a zingy, fresh quaffing drink-me style. Very good value for money.
🧺 Specialist wine stores.

OTHER RED BLENDS AND BRANDED RED WINES

One word says it all about the blended and branded red wines in this year's book: Italy. Nearly everything in that section stands head and shoulders above all the other reds in this chapter, and most are also among the very best wines in this book.

Of course the wine of the year is Spanish, which goes to show that great strides are being made in these so-called Old World wine-producing nations, and this issues a subtle challenge to winemakers in this part of the world that will be hard to beat.

One of the reasons the reds here are so good is that they are made from very old grapevines and another is that they are made from unusual grapes with flavours that cannot be imitated anywhere else.

Be adventurous and give your wine tastebuds a pleasantly surprising workout on these fantastic-value reds.

AUSTRALIA

★★★ **2001 Deen De Bortoli Vat 1 Durif**
$14-15 This earthy Australian red is a good interpretation of the rich fruitcake, gutsy style of wine that Durif is. Good value for money for this fairly rugged style of red.
🍷 *Widely available.*

★★ **1998 Morris Durif**
$19-20 Very meaty Australian red for those who like their steaks rare and their wines big, black and bold.
🍷 *Specialist wine stores.*

★★★ **2000 Pikes Luccio Clare Valley**
$19-20 This medium-bodied red is part of an interesting new-wave Australian red made from 70 percent sangiovese, the classic Tuscan variety in chianti with the balance divided equally between merlot and cabernet sauvignon. Juicy, savoury, loads of interest in flavour in a lightish to medium style.
🍷 *Specialist wine stores nationwide, or for more detail contact Lace Wines, phone (09) 828 4725.*

★★ **2001 Queen Adelaide Regency Red**
$9-10 This is a light, insubstantial Australian red with soft fruit flavours but a slightly bitter finish.
🍷 *Widely available.*

FRANCE

★★★ $9-10
Chateau de la Tuilerie Dinettes et Croustilles Costières de Nimes *(500ml)*
This southern Rhône Valley red is the only French red in the book this year to be sealed with a screwcap. It is made from 95 percent shiraz, 5 percent grenache and is light-bodied and clean, with fresh cherry flavours. Perfect picnic wine in a young, drink-me-right-now style.

🍷 *Specialist wine stores, or contact Wine Direct for a store near you or mail order, freephone 0800 660 777.*

★½ $15-16
1996 Cordier Chateau Tanesse
This wine is past its best, displaying evidence of a formerly pleasing savoury thing that is now, sadly, long gone.

🍷 *New World, specialist wine stores.*

★★★ $19-20
2000 Domaine de la Mordoree Lirac
If this stylish classic label doesn't appeal to you, then the lovely peppery red wine from France's Lirac appellation will. It's soft and smooth with a long, fruity savoury finish. Good value for money.

🍷 *Specialist wine stores, or contact Wine Direct for a store near you or for mail order, freephone 0800 660 777.*

★★★ $11-12
2001 Les Sarments de la Tuilerie
Lovely soft, sweet berry-tasting red from France with a smooth finish and great price tag. Excellent for everyday drinking or tucking into around the fire this winter.

🍷 *Specialist wine stores, or contact Wine Direct for a store near you or mail order, freephone 0800 660 777.*

ITALY

★★½
$17-18

2001 Cecchi Chianti
This is a light Italian red with an earthy and slightly drying finish but interesting savoury flavours, making it a good match with your next steak on the barbecue or bowl of tomato pasta.

🛒 *Glengarry, North Island.*

★★★
$8-9

2001 Citra Montepulciano D'Abruzzo
Lovely juicy little red at an absolutely rock-bottom price with full, fleshy flavours and spice. It's a tad short on the finish but has loads of interesting flavours – sweet fruity, berries, spicy, savoury – and it's a good food wine too.

🛒 *Scenic Cellars, Roberts Street, Taupo, phone (07) 378 5704, email: info@sceniccellars.co.nz*

★★
$12-13

2000 Dario D'Angelo Montepulciano d'Abruzzo
A light Italian red from the Adriatic coast. Spicy but slightly drying on the finish. Average value.

🛒 *Glengarry, North Island.*

★★½
$18-19

1999 Duca di Castelmonte Nero d'Avola
Wild, savoury-tasting red made from an exciting though little-known Italian red grape variety. This is a little rough around the edges but okay value for money and something a bit different. Drink with savoury food.

🛒 *Specialist wine stores, or contact importer Phil Clark at A Touch of Italy for more inforamtion, phone (09) 273 3701, email: sales@touchofitaly.co.nz*

BEST VALUE WINE OF THE YEAR

★★★½
$12-13
2001 Fiorile Rosso Sicilia

This delicious Italian red falls immediately into the category of 'too drinkable'. Its soft Sicilian style makes it the perfect summer-drinking red with its smooth texture, light fruit flavours and lingering velvety finish. It is already great value for money but even better given that a magnum (1.5 litre bottle) costs just $18-19 while the standard 750ml bottle is absolutely unbelievable value. Makes me want to head straight to Sicily! Buy up as much as you can get.

🛒 *Specialist wine stores, or contact importer Phil Clark at A Touch of Italy for more information, phone (09) 273 3701, email: sales@touchofitaly.co.nz*

★★½
$18-20
2001 Frescobaldi Pater Sangiovese

An earthy, interesting-tasting Italian red with a slightly rustic character but lovely flavours of warm fruitiness and spicy, savoury black pepper. Great with a salty pizza.

🛒 *Foodtown, New World, Woolworths and specialist wine stores.*

★★★
$11-12
2001 Lamura Nero d'Avola

This wine is made from the little-known nero d'avola grape variety, from grapes grown in Sicily, which gives it a light, fresh, fruity flavour of surprising depth. It tastes peppery and savoury in an earthy but clean style. And at this price it is excellent value for money. Buy at least a case to enjoy in winter, spring and summer.

🛒 *Specialist wine stores, or contact Wine Direct for a store near you, or for mail order, freephone 0800 660 777.*

★★★
$18-19

2001 Ca Montini La Luna Sangiovese Merlot
Delicious medium-bodied spicy-tasting red blend of sangiovese and merlot grapes. Great value for money and a very food-friendly style.

🛒 *Specialist wine stores, or contact importer Phil Clark at A Touch of Italy for more information, phone (09) 273 3701, email: sales@touchofitaly.co.nz*

★★½
$18-19

2001 Mezza Corona Marzemino
A soft, sweet Italian red with a light body and spicy-tasting finish.

🛒 *Specialist wine stores, or contact importer Phil Clark at A Touch of Italy for more information, phone (09) 273 3701, email: sales@touchofitaly.co.nz*

★★½
$18-19

2001 Mezza Corona Teroldego Rotaliano
Lovely sweet and savoury red wine made in the Trentino region in the north of Italy. This wine has a smooth texture and medium body and length. Very good value for money.

🛒 *Specialist wine stores, or contact importer Phil Clark at A Touch of Italy for more information, phone (09) 273 3701, email: sales@touchofitaly.co.nz*

★★★½
$17-18

2001 Norante Di Majo Sangiovese
Gorgeous quaffer and classically good Italian sangiovese. Has very good sweet, clean sort of leather/savoury aromas and flavours. Excellent value. Hints of licorice, black pepper and sweet fruit.

🛒 *Caro's Wines, Ponsonby Road, Auckland.*

★★½
$12-13

2000 Pasqua Bardolino Classico
This Italian red is good value for money, offering up light and extremely attractive tastes of earthy, savoury herbs and fresh wildberry fruit flavours.
Widely available.

★★★½
$18-19

2000 Pasqua & Fazio Wines of Sicily Nero D'Avola Cabernet Sauvignon
An unusual blend for Sicily, but definitely the best, juiciest and cleanest by far of all the wines tasted at the bench today from Italy – seven wines in all. This wine has explosive juicy flavours from the nero d'avola that are given good back-up from the staunch cabernet sauvignon.
Glengarry, North Island.

★★★
$18-19

2000 Pasqua Lapaccio Primitivo Salento
This red from southern Italy is made from the primitivo grape variety and oak-aged to give it a clean, earthy appeal. Would be perfect with a bowl of meaty pasta. And it is great value for money.
Glengarry, North Island.

★★★
$12-13

2000 Pasqua Valpolicella Classico
This cherry-tasting, herby Italian red is very good value for money and offers wine drinkers a great alternative to cab sauv and shiraz by being juicy, light and savoury in taste. Buy lots and enjoy it with your next meaty pasta dish.
Widely available.

WINERY OF THE YEAR

★★★½
$19-20

2001 Promessa Negroamaro

This red from southern Italy has the most intensely wild blackberry flavours, a spicy, even slightly licorice hint and a savoury, lingering finish. Buy at least a couple of bottles, because this is so tasty that's how much you'll want. Fantastic value for money.

♛ *Specialist wine stores, or contact Bennett & Deller Wine Merchantsfor stores near you, phone (09) 378 9463.*

★★★½
$19-20

2001 Promessa Rosso Salento

A luscious, fantastically perfumed quaffing red from Puglia in the south of Italy. It's made from two grapes: negroamaro and primitivo, which team up to make for a flavoursome, surprisingly soft and delicious red. Earthy, savoury tastes combine with fruit to make one of the best reds under $20 available in New Zealand.

♛ *Specialist wine stores, or contact Bennett & Deller Wine Merchants for stores near you, phone (09) 378 9463.*

★★½
$16-17

2001 Renzo Masi Chianti

Light-bodied and basic quaffing Italian red. Average value.

♛ *Specialist wine stores, or contact importer Phil Clark at A Touch of Italy for more information, phone (09) 273 3701, email: sales@touchofitaly.co.nz*

★★½
$18-19

2000 Rivera Rupicolo
Light and fruity Italian red with a shortish finish but a lovely combination of earthy and sweet cherry flavours. Good – no, make that very good – with flavoursome pizza, crusty and crisp and Italian-style.

Specialist wine stores, or contact importer Phil Clark at A Touch of Italy for more information, phone (09) 273 3701, email: sales@touchofitaly.co.nz

★★★½
$17-18

2001 Rocca delle Macie Vernaiolo Chianti DOCG
This delicious soft, savoury-tasting chianti is great value and so drinkable and lingering at the finish it'll have you onto a second glass. Team it up with good prosciutto and you have a hard-to-beat combination.

Specialist wine stores, or contact Vintners New Zealand for stockists near you, phone (09) 979 2900, email: vintnersnz.co.nz

★★½
$13-14

2000 Umani Ronchi Montepulciano D'Abruzzo
If you are willing to venture beyond the boundaries of Australian shiraz, then try this light, savoury-tasting Italian red with its white pepper and spice with a hint of plums. Tasty but very light and good value for interesting everyday drinking.

Specialist wine stores, or contact Vintners New Zealand for stockists near you, phone (09) 979 2900, email: vintnersnz.co.nz

★★★½
$18-19

1999 Umani Ronchi San Lorenzo Rosso Conero
I have always loved the savoury flavours and iron-fist-in-a-velvet-glove style of this spicy Italian red. It's perfect with pasta but this is a relatively robust red that can impress you on its own merits without the decoy that food provides. A meaty, velvety finish that lingers.

Specialist wine stores, or contact Vintners New Zealand for stockists near you, phone (09) 979 2900, email: vintnersnz.co.nz

★★★ **2001 Umani Ronchi Serrano**
$17-18 Interesting Italian red with lots of extract. This is a big wine which will either woo or turn you off with its full-on, almost Australian-styled big, fruity flavours and medium-length finish. Impressive if size is what counts.
Specialist wine stores, or contact Vintners New Zealand for stockists near you, phone (09) 979 2900, email: vintnersnz.co.nz

NEW ZEALAND

★★½ **Nobilo Fernleaf Vintage Red**
$10-11 The words 'vintage red' in the name may confuse wine drinkers, especially as this wine has no vintage, meaning that it's made with grapes grown in a combination of different years. It is a lovely zingy style of red made mostly from pinotage grapes with some cabernet sauvignon thrown in for good measure too. Good-value barbecue red, even if the name is slightly confusing.
Widely available.

★½ **Wohnseidler Classic Red**
$6-7 Simple, light red but far superior to the white in this range – and drier too. It's cheap but it's okay, in a sweetish sort of way.
Widely available.

SPAIN

WINE OF THE YEAR

★★★★
$14-16

2001 Carchelo Jumilla
Stunning every year but especially good this time with a particularly soft red from Spain's 2001 vintage. This is just one of the ripples in the tidal wave of fresh, new-styled Spanish wines. It is soft from the first whiff, simultaneously sensuous and earthy in taste. Delicious stuff and fantastic value for money.
  Specialist wine stores, or contact Eurowine, phone (09) 636 4045.

★★★
$14-15

1998 Gran Colegiata Crianza Farina
Like so many Spanish wines across a range of prices today, this one boasts surprisingly fresh, fruity flavours. It is held tightly together in an oaky-tasting package and has medium length. Good value for money and worth venturing outside of your comfort zone to find.
  Specialist wine stores, or contact Wine Direct for a store near you or for mail order, freephone 0800 660 777.

★★★
$12-13

2000 LAN Rioja Gran Dominio *(500ml)*
This brilliantly convenient new 500ml bottle contains a sweet leathery, distinctively traditional-styled rioja. I like its earthy, sweet style. The wine is made mainly of tempranillo with 20 percent grenache in the blend.
  Wine Direct, Newmarket, Auckland or freephone 0800 660 777.

SOUTH AFRICA

★★ **2001 Drostdy-Hof Cape Red**
$13-14 A very light, warm, friendly little South African red. This wine offers simple quaffing, which will appeal greatly to new wine drinkers. At this price it is average value for money.

🛒 *The Mill Liquorsave; Scenic Cellars, Roberts Street, Taupo or contact Burleigh Trading for more stockists, phone (09) 480 0789.*

PINOTAGE

Pinotage is a crossing of the grape varieties pinot noir and cinsault, created by Professor A I Perold in 1925 at Stellenbosch University in South Africa. Plantings of pinotage in South Africa increased in the 1990s so that it now accounts for about 3 percent of that country's vineyard area. Pinotage also increased in popularity in New Zealand in the 1990s, going from 52 hectares in 1991 to 87 hectares in 2003.

★★★½ **2002 Babich East Coast Pinotage Cabernet**
$13-14
Babich Wines has been making good pinotage for what seems like forever. This version has a bit more backbone than most, which must be due at least partly to the addition of cabernet sauvignon that adds weight to the wine. Good value for money.
🛒 *Widely available.*

★★ **1999 Bellingham Pinotage**
$17-18
At three years old this South African pinotage is now fading just a tad, lacking the vibrant freshness that good pinotage is all about but still offering earthy, oaky and spicy flavours. Team it up with a good steak on the barbecue.
🛒 *Liquor stores and supermarkets, or contact Federal Geo for stockists, phone (09) 578 1823, email: federalgeo@xtra.co.nz*

★★★½ **2002 Lincoln Winemakers Series Gisborne Pinotage**
$14-15
Here is yet another example of great-value purple-coloured, wildberry-tasting pinotage. Fantastic value for money and so deliciously fruity but clean and earthy at the same time. Great buying.
🛒 *Liquorland and Cellar Select, or contact Lincoln Vineyards, phone (09) 838 6944, email: wine@lincolnwines.co.nz*

★★
$11-12

2002 Matua Settler Pinotage Cabernet Sauvignon

This blend of sweet pinotage with staunch cabernet sauvignon is a little lean on fruit warmth. The cabernet sauvignon berry flavours taste a tad green in this wine, which is decent value for money for a basic red everyday drinking wine.

Widely available.

★★★
$16-17

2001 Saints Pinotage

Clean, fresh, almost explosively shirazy, fruity note. Deliciously easy to enjoy and very good value for money.

Widely available.

★★★
$14-15

2001 Sanctuary Marlborough Pinotage/Pinot Noir

I like this inventive combination of two relatively early-ripening grapes which give a wine oozing fresh, light cherry flavours. It has medium length and represents great value for money for a summer quaffing red in a light but fresh style.

Most supermarkets and some specialist wine stores.

★★
$14-16

2002 Trapiche Pinot Noir

A warm, fresh Argentinian pinot noir with sweet cherry flavours and a slightly drying finish.

Widely available.

PINOT NOIR

Pinot noir is New Zealand's most planted red grape variety with more than three times the amount of pinot noir vines in the ground as cabernet sauvignon and more than double the amount of merlot (the country's second largest grape variety). Consequently, most of the pinot noir in this chapter is from New Zealand, although a substantial portion of the pinot noir planted in this country is also used to produce quality sparkling wine.

Pinot noir's home is Burgundy, France, where it is responsible for some of the world's most acclaimed – and highly priced – red wines. It grows best in cool grape-growing climates such as Burgundy, Oregon in the United States, and New Zealand. Pinot noir is prone to mutate, which is how the pinot gris, pinot blanc and pinot meunier grapes came into being.

★★★
$14-16

2001 Babich East Coast Pinot Noir
This is a good introduction to pinot noir for lovers of big reds. It's light and smooth, cherry-tasting and very slightly spicy. My only gripe is the short, slightly drying finish. Otherwise this is good value, clean and fresh and, most importantly, it's easy to enjoy.

🛒 *Widely available.*

★★
$17-18

2000 Bourgogne Passetoutgrain Jean-Marc Brocard
This very light red is made from the pinot noir grape but it is too light and lacks fruit flavour.

🛒 *Chateauneuf store, 48 Pollen Street, Ponsonby, Auckland or by mail order, phone (09) 378 7011, email: Chateauneuf@xtra.co.nz*

★★★
$17-19

2000 Collards Queen Charlotte Pinot Noir
This is very light but pleasantly toasty pinot noir made from grapes grown in Marlborough. Its aim is to appeal to a wide and large audience at an affordable price, which it achieves with its light, fresh style.

🛒 *Widely available, or from Collards winery, phone (09) 838 8341.*

★★½
$16-17

2002 Coopers Creek Pinot Noir
Very light ruby-coloured pinot that finishes quickly at the end of each mouthful with light fresh flavours but not much body or length.

🛒 *Most wine stores and supermarkets nationwide.*

★★
$17-18

2001 Corbans Stoneleigh Marlborough Pinot Noir
There's a dried-out fruity thing happening here which carries through to the palate where the fruit is not very intense and the texture is a little hard. Average.

🛒 *Widely available.*

★★★½ 2002 Drylands Marlborough Pinot Noir
$18-19

Excellent-value pinot noir made with grapes grown in Marlborough. This is one of the fruitiest, freshest and purest of all the pinots in this year's guide. Excellent value for an under-$20 pinot noir.

🛒 *Widely available.*

★★½ 2000 Georges Duboeuf Pinot Noir Vin de Pays D'Oc
$16-17

This is a tasty little pinot noir from the south of France, with spicy earthy flavours in a distinctly different style to the pinot noirs at this price from this part of the world. It's flavoursome but light-bodied, which is exactly what is called for in mid-summer or autumn. Good value for money.

🛒 *Glengarry, North Island.*

★★★ 2000 Joseph Drouhin Laforet
$19-20

As the everyday red of Domaine Joseph Drouhin in Burgundy, France, this is pretty tasty stuff. It's light but characteristically pinot noir-tasting in style with its cherry flavours and savoury, light peppery finish. This is good value for money too.

🛒 *Specialist wine stores, or contact Wine Direct for a store near you or for mail order, freephone 0800 660 777.*

★★½ 2002 Kim Crawford Hawke's Bay Pinot Noir
$19-20

Light in colour, aroma and flavour but streets ahead of where this wine used to be when it was sealed with a horrible, oxidative plastic stopper. This is zingy and acidic and fresh; would be great with the right food.

🛒 *Glengarry, North Island, and specialist wine stores nationwide.*

★★★ **1998 Maison Chandesais Bourgogne Pinot Noir**
$19-20 Lovely, tasty French pinot noir. This everyday drinking red wine tastes of fresh cherries and spice. It is very good value for money, delivering a flavoursome style of pinot noir with balance and elegance in a light style.
🛒 *Chateauneuf store, 48 Pollen Street, Ponsonby, Auckland or by mail order, phone (09) 378 7011, email: Chateauneuf@xtra.co.nz*

★★½ **2002 Montana Marlborough Pinot Noir**
$15-16 This is one of the lightest pinot noirs around that still has flavours of vibrant, fresh cherries held in a light spicy wine. Good entry-level pinot noir.
🛒 *Widely available.*

★★½ **2001 Preece Pinot Noir**
$17-18 This Australian pinot noir is all cherries and dried herbs in flavour. It's silky smooth in texture and even slightly lingering at the finish. Light but hugely enjoyable.
🛒 *Liquor King and specialist wine stores.*

★★½ **2001 Queen Adelaide Pinot Noir**
$9-10 This well-known Australian wine brand often provides great value for money but pinot noir at a low price presents more of a challenge than most grapes. I like the fresh cherry fruity flavours in this wine but it is, as the price tag suggests, a simple everyday drink.
🛒 *Widely available.*

★★★ **2001 Rosemount Estate Pinot Noir**
$15-16 Bright red Australian pinot noir that tastes like sweet, soft grenache with a kick of oak at the finish. This is a light-bodied little red but very easy to drink; perfect for summer with pink steak.
🛒 *Widely available.*

★★★ 2002 Shingle Peak Marlborough Pinot Noir
$18-19

A lovely fresh, wild-berry-tasting pinot noir with hints of sweet cocoa flavour about it and a soft texture. It's a stand-alone wine which might fit in with roast chicken or duck but tastes just fab on its own. A lovely red spicy, fruity, soft-drinking wine that will impress you and your friends or family with its robust medium body and flavour.

Widely available.

★★½ 2001 Stoneleigh Pinot Noir
$19-20
A dried-out, fruity thing happening here carries through to the palate where the fruit is not very intense and the texture is a little hard.

Widely available.

★★★ 2001 Tasman Bay Nelson Pinot Noir
$19-20
Lovely, incredibly easy-to-drink young pinot noir that is fantastically fresh and sweet. There is a spicy flavour here but it's more of a ripe, sweet red-black cherry-tasting pinot noir. Fantastic – especially at the price!

Widely available or contact Spencer Hill winery, phone (03) 543 2031, email: male@tasmanbaywine.com

★★ 2001 Taylors Estate Pinot Noir
$18-19
Very light cherry-tasting Australian pinot noir that is astringent on the finish and lacks substance. Has a hard edge to the finish.

Widely available.

★★ 2001 Twin Islands Pinot Noir
$18-19
Incredibly light red with soft, creamy texture. Average value for money.

Big Fresh, Woolworths, specialist wine stores.

2001 Tyrrell's Old Winery Pinot Noir

★★
$15-16

The famous Tyrrell's winery in Australia's Hunter Valley, just north of Sydney, is better known for its shiraz than its pinot noir. This is a lively cherry-coloured pinot noir with light, fresh flavours and a slightly short finish.

Widely available.

2001 Wai-iti River Vineyard Nelson Pinot Noir

★★½
$19-20

This Nelson pinot noir has lovely bright-red cherry colours, with purity of pinot noir flavour and a delicious earthy hint. Spicy and delicious and medium to light.

Seriously Fine Wines and St Helier's Wines, or mail order from Woollaston Estates winery, phone (03) 542 3205, email: wine@WollastonEstates.co.nz

2001 Windy Peak Pinot Noir

★★
$17-18

Very light, drying red with a slightly spicy sweet taste.

Glengarry, North Island; New World, nationwide.

2001 Wyndham Estate Bin 333 Pinot Noir

★★½
$14-15

Very light Australian pinot noir that is average value for money but soft in texture and flavour and easy to enjoy in the sunshine. This is definitely a daytime wine.

Widely available.

SANGIOVESE

Sangiovese is Italy's most planted grape variety and is made into everything from cheap and cheerful to brilliant chianti.

Sangiovese means 'blood of Jove', according to *Jancis Robinson's Guide to Wine Grapes*, and the grape is thought to be indigenous not only to Italy but specifically to Tuscany.

It is grown in small quantities in New Zealand and in larger degree with more success in Australia. The sangiovese grape mutates easily, which is one reason for varying qualities of wine made from this grape.

★★½
$14-15

2000 Renzo Masi Sangiovese

Light, simple red made from Italy's best-known red grape, sangiovese. This wine has more than a hint of earthiness about its flavour which is balanced by a light fruity taste, but a short finish lets it down just a tad. Average value.

🛒 *Specialist wine stores, or contact importer Phil Clark at A Touch of Italy for more information, phone (09) 273 3701, email: sales@touchofitaly.co.nz*

SHIRAZ AND SYRAH

It's no surprise to find more wines in this chapter than any other red wine category with the continuing growth in the amount of Australian shiraz available in New Zealand, and most of it unbelievably affordable. For all that, the quality of the wines featured in this chapter is a roller-coaster ride with exhilaratingly zingy highs and some pretty scary lows. Not just from Australia, of course. Shiraz and syrah are different names for the same red grape variety and the difference between them is stylistic. Shiraz is usually a bolder, more fruit-driven wine; syrah is usually spicier and earthier, as the wines here from France and a smattering of other countries show.

It is easy to be wooed by the big, bold Aussie versions, but don't overlook the lighter styles which are often easier to enjoy because they are more subtle in taste and work better with food. They are often easier on the system, too, since a couple of glasses won't give you the heady rush you'll get from many high-alcohol Australian shirazes.

★★½　**2001 Ashwood Grove Shiraz**
$15-16　This is a pretty light little Aussie shiraz with simple fruit flavours and a light finish.

Hamilton Wine Company; Munslow's Wines, Dunedin; Wanaka Fine Wines, Central Otago; or contact Burleigh Trading for more stockists, phone (09) 480 0789.

★★★　**2002 Banrock Station Shiraz**
$14-16　The little gold sticker on each bottle of this wine doesn't indicate that it has won an award but rather that every time you buy a bottle of Banrock Station shiraz some of the profit goes towards restoring and preserving wetlands in New Zealand. The wine itself is more than worthy of supporting, too, not least because it has such an accessible price tag. Its flavours are light but sweetly appealing, with fresh plummy tastes and a lingering, slightly spicy finish. Great value for money.

Widely available.

★★½　**2001 Banrock Station Shiraz Cabernet**
$9-10　This is a consistently good value red wine. The value comes into play here because this is a rock-bottom price for a wine that oozes flavour, balance and a texture verging on lusciously silky. It ends on a slightly drying note but you will enjoy the flavour (and price) so much that it hardly matters for an everyday red like this.

Widely available.

★★½　**2001 Beacon Hill Shiraz Cabernet**
$13-14　A light fruity wine with some nice mid-palate weight and not over-the-top sweet fruit flavour but a slightly simple, short, raw finish.

Specialist wine stores nationwide, or for more detail contact Lace Wines, phone (09) 828 4725.

★★½
$17-18

2000 Bellingham Shiraz
This is an earthy, distinctively savoury South African shiraz, big and bold but less fruity than the obvious Aussie styles. Average value for money at this price.

Where to buy: Liquor stores and supermarkets, or contact Federal Geo for stockists, phone (09) 578 1823, email: federalgeo@xtra.co.nz

★★★
$18-19

2001 Beresford Highwood McLaren Vale Shiraz
Sweet fruit and savoury bacon flavours combine in this delicious light, spicy Australian shiraz, which offers loads of flavour and interest in this price range. It would even work well with a savoury homemade beef and wine pie. Good value.

Specialist wine stores nationwide, or for more detail contact Lace Wines, phone (09) 828 4725.

★★½
$14-16

2000 Cheviot Bridge Shiraz
This medium-bodied shiraz is made with grapes grown in South Australia and it has hints of spicy flavour and a touch of juicy plums in taste, hinting at what great Aussie shiraz is all about.

Glengarry, North Island; other specialist wine stores; or contact Marcus Pickens at Hancocks, phone (09) 379 3740.

★★★
$17-19

2000 Collards Marlborough Syrah
This spicy little Marlborough red is deliciously good value for money, offering oodles of freshness and flavoursome juicy plummy tastes. This is great-value drinking, which shows exactly why syrah is often referred to as poor man's pinot noir.

Widely available, or from Collards winery, phone (09) 838 8341.

1999 Comte de Peyrevive Crozes Hermitage

★★ $19-20

A rather lean French syrah that is only average value for money with its light body and thin flavours.

🛒 *Chateauneuf store, 48 Pollen Street, Ponsonby, Auckland or by mail order, phone (09) 378 7011, email: Chateauneuf@xtra.co.nz*

2001 Cookoothama Darlington Point Shiraz

★★½ $16-17

Tastes like essence of blackberry. This is warm, flavoursome red wine but needs a hearty fire to go with it. Definitely winter wine.

🛒 *Specialist wine stores.*

2001 Corbans Shiraz

★★ $13-14

This cool-climate shiraz style would be better if it were not so green in aroma, which also carries through in the sappy finish and lean flavour.

🛒 *Widely available.*

2002 Corbans White Label Shiraz

★★ $8-9

Lighter in style and body than most shirazes in the book this year so average value for money.

🛒 *Widely available.*

2001 Cottlers Bridge Shiraz

★★★ $9-10

Superior by a long way to the rest in this range, with sweet fruity flavours of lightly stewed plums with a spicy addition and a dryish finish. Great value for money.

🛒 *Cellar Select and Wine Masters, Auckland; Advintage, Hastings. For South Island sales, contact Wine Masters, phone (09) 636 5240.*

★★★ 2001 Deakin Estate Shiraz
$13–14

As one of the few Australian shirazes in this price range to have sweet, rich, ripe flavours, this is excellent value for money. It even lingers a little at the finish, giving it an extra appeal.

Widely available.

★★ 2001 De Bortoli Shiraz
$17–18

This is a light, simple shiraz with basic fruit flavour but a very short finish. Pretty average wine. Take it to a barbecue.

Glengarry, North Island; other specialist wine stores; or contact Marcus Pickens at Hancocks, phone (09) 379 3740.

★★½ 2000 Eaglehawk Shiraz Merlot Cabernet
$12–13

Simple, sherbety, zingy red blend of shiraz, merlot and cabernet grapes. This wine lacks focus somewhat but offers a good basic-level drinking red.

Widely available.

★★½ 2001 Firestick Langhorne Creek Shiraz Cabernet Sauvignon
$18–19

Fresh and fruity with flavours of raspberry and soft, sweet, red fleshy plum. Deliciously easy to drink. Okay value for money.

Macvine, phone (03) 570 2118.

★★ 2000 Four Sisters Trevor Mast Shiraz
$19–20

Very light and simple shiraz with a definite taste of strawberry jam and little else to commend it. Drying and short finish.

Specialist wine stores nationwide, or for more detail contact Lace Wines, phone (09) 828 4725.

★★★ **2001 Goldridge Estate Matakana**
$15-16 **Shiraz Merlot Cabernet**
Excellent value. This is a juicy, tasty little number made from blending shiraz, merlot and cabernet sauvignon grapes, all of which were grown at Matakana, an hour's drive north of Auckland. The result of the blend is the juicy, sweet and instant appeal of shiraz coupled with the softness of merlot and backbone of cabernet.
🍷 *Foodtown, specialist wine stores and liquor retailers.*

★★ **2001 Hanging Rock Shiraz Grenache &**
$15-16 **Pinot Noir**
Love the look of the simple red label and stopper! The wine itself tastes a little thin and plain and represents below-average value.
🍷 *Glengarry, North Island; other specialist wine stores; or contact Marcus Pickens at Hancocks, phone (09) 379 3740.*

★★★ **Hardys Shiraz Mataro**
$8-9 Good value for money for a soft, easy-to-enjoy, basic everyday quaffing red. It's made from the well-known shiraz grape, which is blended with the lesser-known mataro.
🍷 *Widely available.*

★★★ **2001 Hardys Varietal Range Shiraz**
$8-9 Instantly recognisable, sweet, jammy Australian shiraz. Good value for money for a tasty, drink-alone (rather than with food) wine.
🍷 *Widely available.*

★★½ **1998 Henry Lawson Mudgee Shiraz**
$19-20
This is a very port-like Australian shiraz with intense, rich fruity flavours and a hot finish but with an appealing immediate flavour that will draw drinkers into enjoying it.
🧺 *Specialist wine stores.*

★★ **2000 Houghton Shiraz**
$15-16
This Western Australian red is very light in style and a tad one-dimensional with drying, vaguely red-plum flavours.
🧺 *Widely available.*

★★★ **Jackman Ridge Shiraz Cabernet**
$8-9
Meaty and robust and far better than many wines at this price. Light and fresh and simple but clean and lovely; easy to like because it tastes like wine rather than cheap oak tricks.
🧺 *Widely available.*

★★★½ **2000 Jacob's Creek Reserve Shiraz**
$19-20
If you're looking for a wine to tuck away for a few years, try this. Buy half a case and drink a bottle every six months to see how it evolves in flavour. It's like dark chocolate, a very rich fruity shiraz with hints of black pepper and a gutsy body. This is young and tasty but needs time to soften out.
🧺 *Widely available.*

★★ **2000 Jacob's Creek Shiraz**
$11-12
This is a very light, sherbety shiraz with freshness but a short finish.
🧺 *Widely available.*

★★½ 2001 Kingston Shiraz
$15-16

Very light-tasting Australian shiraz with hints of spice but only average value for money.

🛒 *Fine Wine Delivery Company, Auckland; Munslow's, Dunedin; or contact Burleigh Trading for more stockists, phone (09) 480 0789.*

★★★½ 2001 Leasingham Bastion Clare Valley Shiraz Cabernet Sauvignon
$19-20

This sweet, juicy, great-value Australian red is an elegant wine. A blend of shiraz and cabernet sauvignon grapes that combine for a well-balanced wine. Buy at least half a case.

🛒 *Widely available.*

★★★ 2001 Lindemans Bin 50 Shiraz
$12-13

Lovely sweet, rich Australian shiraz that is packed with intensely concentrated plum flavours, medium body and good length. It tastes like black, freshly picked plums, just as you would expect of a good Aussie shiraz.

🛒 *Widely available.*

★★★ 2000 Lindemans Cawarra Shiraz Cabernet
$9-10

Very drinkable, surprisingly balanced blend of shiraz and cabernet sauvignon grapes. And while this wine doesn't ooze over-the-top concentration of flavour, it is nicely in tune with the style and price, offering an easy but flavoursome drop. Great value.

🛒 *Widely available.*

★★★ 2001 Lindemans Reserve South Australia Shiraz
$18-19

Great-value warm and very flavoursome shiraz that tastes of juicy black plums mixed with a handful of sweet spice and a touch of aniseed. All these tastes come together in an appealing red style that offers very good value for money.

Widely available.

★★★ 2000 McPherson's Shiraz
$13-14

Lovely sweet fruity shiraz in that instantly recognisably Australian style with generous fruit.

Liquor stores and supermarkets, or contact Federal Geo for stockists, phone (09) 578 1823, email: federalgeo@xtra.co.nz

★★ 2000 McPherson's Shiraz Cabernet
$13-14

Very light and fresh, almost like a thinnish style of Beaujolais. Light-bodied, average-value everyday drinking red.

Liquor stores and supermarkets, or contact Federal Geo for stockists, phone (09) 578 1823, email: federalgeo@xtra.co.nz

★★★½ 2000 Maglieri of McLaren Vale Shiraz
$18-20

This is a deliciously intense, purely shiraz-tasting shiraz. It is spicy and rich in flavour without ever overwhelming the tastebuds. I like its intensity of taste and the smooth way it just seems to glide down the throat, urging you on to take another sip to see if it really is as good as it seems. The answer is a resounding yes. Buy heaps!

Widely available.

★★
$14-15

2001 Manara Rock Shiraz
This is a fresh new wine brand in New Zealand – arrived on our shores in October 2002. This is instantly recognisable Australian shiraz with plummy, fruity flavours but a very light style. It's good value for everyday quaffing in the sun but lacks the guts of a big winter red.
Widely available.

★★½
$8-10

2001 Mathew Lang Shiraz Cabernet
Incredibly light, red Aussie blend of shiraz and cabernet. This wine lacks flavour and body.
Widely available.

★★★
$16-17

2000 Michel Laroche Syrah
A light red from the south of France with lovely fresh, warm, earthy flavours at the finish and a sweet but not fruit-driven style. This is refreshingly different in style – clean, slightly savoury, with hints of black pepper taste. Good value.
Specialist wine stores.

★★★½
$19-20

2001 Moculta Shiraz
Intense Aussie shiraz with deliciously deep, sweet black-plum flavours and a dry finish. I like the style of this big, bold red, which is not over-the-top. My only complaint is that it finishes on a very slightly astringent note, otherwise this is very good value for money.
Widely available.

★★★ 2001 Montana Shiraz
$14-15

'Produce of Australia' is written clearly on the label of this New Zealand-branded Montana varietals wine in the bottle with the clumpy bottom. And a rather nice, juicy drop it is too.

🛒 *Widely available.*

★★★ 2002 Murray Ridge Shiraz Cabernet
$9-10

This zingy, fresh, shiraz-dominant red has to be one of the best-value reds under $10 available in New Zealand right now. It is not a wine that the buffs would refer to as complex, but it does deliver plenty of softness in texture, spiciness of flavour and lovely fresh fruity tastes of ripe black plums and berries. Very good value.

🛒 *Widely available.*

★★½ 2000 Nottage Hill Shiraz
$11-12

This lovely, bargain-bin shiraz towers above the other Nottage Hill reds in flavour and value for money. It is sweet and explosively juicy in style but finishes on a dryish note. Good value.

🛒 *Widely available.*

★★ 2001 Pauletts Stone Cutting Shiraz Cabernet Malbec
$19-20

This has a minty thing going on from the cabernet which also tastes a little stalky in this wine but otherwise it's okay. Pretty average stuff for the price; a bit hard and grippy at the finish.

🛒 *Specialist wine stores nationwide, or for more detail contact Lace Wines, phone (09) 828 4725.*

★★★½ 2001 Penfolds Koonunga Hill Shiraz Cabernet
$17-18

Very concentrated Australian red that is definitely one of the best buys in this chapter and in the book. Big, bold, spicy and fruity but not over-the-top in style. This is multi-layered and incredibly youthful still, needing time to unfold its peppery shiraz flavours and blackberry cabernet taste.

Widely available.

★★½ 2002 Penfolds Rawson's Retreat Shiraz Cabernet
$13-14

It might be the lowest-tier red in the mighty Penfolds wine stable, but this is a surprisingly tasty little blend of shiraz and cabernet. It's mainly the shiraz that gives this wine its sweet richness and gutsy style. Good value for money.

Widely available.

★★★½ 2001 Penfolds Thomas Hyland Shiraz
$19-20

This wine is easily the top red of the new Thomas Hyland range of wines, launched late last year. And, while it is instantly recognisable as Australian with jammy sweet flavours, I also like its medium body and the fact that it is a significant step up in flavour from the always good Koonunga Hill.

Widely available.

★★★ 2001 Peter Lehmann Clancy's
$18-19

Medium ruby-red blend of shiraz, cabernet sauvignon and merlot grapes grown in the heat-filled Barossa Valley, Australia. It has a slightly minty aroma on the nose and loads of lovely sweet cinnamon and nutmeg spicy flavours wrapped in a plummy texture with juicy qualities too. Good-value red with more depth and length than many in this price range.

Big Fresh, Foodtown, Woolworths, specialist wine stores.

★★★½ 2000 Preece Shiraz
$17-18

This is one tasty shiraz with vibrant juicy flavours mid-palate and a take-me-by-surprise savoury taste, too, adding delicious interest to its ripe, sweet plummy taste. Great value for money.

Liquor King, specialist wine stores.

★★½ 2001 Queen Adelaide Shiraz
$9-10

Very light but lovely, soft, savoury-tasting shiraz with hints of fresh herbs like thyme and even a taste of aniseed about it. This is very good value for money.

Widely available.

★★★½ 2000 Redbank Fighting Flat King Valley Shiraz
$19-20

This is big but elegant and juicy shiraz with fresh, fleshy fruit flavours in an impeccably clean style, but it needs time to open up. By the time this book is out it will be doing just that, meaning this impressive red is great value for money, just sneaking into this guide.

Specialist wine stores.

★★★
$14-15

2000 Redbank Long Paddock Shiraz Cabernet Sauvignon
Fresh, zingy, cherry-flavoured red in a very light shiraz style but still medium weight with lovely fruit and life. Clean and tasty for above-average everyday quaffing.
🧺 *Specialist wine stores.*

★★★½
$19-20

2000 Richmond Grove Barossa Shiraz
Brilliant buying, this intensely plummy and ripe-tasting shiraz. It is one of the best wines of the book both in quality and value for money, delivering a relatively full-bodied and impressively lingering taste for the price. Buy a case.
🧺 *Specialist wine stores.*

★★★
$10-11

2001 Robard & Butler Shiraz
Fresh and fruity but a little hard on the finish. Still, it has robust fruit flavours, despite the oaky tannic finish. Good value at this amazing price. It would stand up well to a rare steak.
🧺 *Widely available.*

★★½
$15-16

2001 Rosemount Estate Shiraz
Drinkable, good-value Australian shiraz in a softer than usual style, made for drinking every day without too much analysing.
🧺 *Widely available.*

★★
$12-13

2002 Rosemount Estate Shiraz Cabernet
A light, insubstantial Australian red blend of shiraz and cabernet sauvignon grapes. Average.
🧺 *Widely available.*

★★★ 2001 St Hallett Gamekeepers Reserve
$18-19

Soft, spicy red but a little astringent, although loads of people will love the raspberry flavours and spicy sweetness of this tasty little number.

🍷 *Glengarry, Liquor King, Liquorland, specialist wine stores.*

★★½ 2001 Saints Vineyard Selection Shiraz
$16-17

'Produce of Australia' is written in proud print on the bottom of the front label, which is as it should be. This is soft and fruity, easy to enjoy without the complexity of many of the shirazes featured here.

🍷 *Widely available.*

★★★ 2000 Salena Estate South Australia Shiraz
$16-17

Here is a lovely ripe, rich plummy-tasting shiraz from South Australia. It has loads of black fleshy, plummy flavour in the mid-palate and has a lingering, sexy finish. Excellent value for money and loads of flavour.

🍷 *Specialist wine stores, or contact Vintners New Zealand for stockists near you, phone (09) 979 2900, email: vintnersnz.co.nz*

★★★ 2001 Sandalford Element Shiraz Cabernet
$15-16

This Western Australian wine is a light blend of shiraz and cabernet sauvignon grapes. It has fresh, sweet fruit flavours and a slightly short finish. Average value at this price.

🍷 *Wine Masters, Auckland; Liquorland, Feilding; Vino Fino, Christchurch; The Mill Liquorsave; or contact Burleigh Trading for more stockists, phone (09) 480 0789.*

2001 Silky Oak Shiraz

★★½ $12-13

Another great-value red in the Silky Oak range. This one has sweet flavours of red plums and a light spicy finish. Good buying for everyday drinking.

🛒 *Liquor stores and supermarkets, or contact Federal Geo for stockists, phone (09) 578 1823, email: federalgeo@xtra.co.nz*

2000 Stepping Stone Shiraz

★★★ $14-15

This is one of the winners in this chapter with bold Australian shiraz flavours of sweet plums and spice. Like the other two reds in this Stonehaven range, this one is made with grapes grown in vineyards on the Limestone Coast in South Australia. This wine is purplish black in colour with soft, sweet, juicy flavours and a lovely silky styled texture. Great value for money.

🛒 *Widely available.*

2001 Taylors Estate Shiraz

★★★½ $18-19

Here is an explosively juicy, deliciously ripe, brilliant-tasting red. It's soft and sweet with backbone and spice. Flavours run the gamut of Damson plums to aniseed and even a touch of black pepper, and if your imagination doesn't stretch to those crazy adjectival limits, then just pour yourself a glass and enjoy.

🛒 *Widely available.*

2001 Taylors Promised Land Shiraz Cabernet

★★★½ $14-15

Like its name, this is an extremely promising and rich-tasting Australian red made from shiraz and cabernet sauvignon grapes. It tastes exactly as you want a sweet, plummy-tasting dark-coloured red wine to. The finish is lingering and full.

🛒 *Widely available.*

★★★½ **2001 Thorn-Clarke Sandpiper Barossa Shiraz**
$19-20

A lovely juicy Australian shiraz with very lingering, impressively tasty finish that is at the same time plummy and sweet and savoury and earthy. Fantastic value for money. Buy it by the caseload and love it this winter.

🛒 *Huapai Wines & Spirits, Auckland; Munslow's, Dunedin; or contact Burleigh Trading for more stockists, phone (09) 480 0789.*

★★½ **2001 Timara Oak Aged Shiraz**
$9-10

Basic everyday quaffing shiraz with nicely integrated oak flavour but a slightly grippy finish. Not bad value.

🛒 *Widely available.*

★★★ **1997 Trapiche Syrah**
$18-19

This Argentinian syrah is a flavour-packed, powerful red tasting of black ripe, sweet, succulent plums. It has a hint of savoury, earthy spice and medium body. It is great value for money and also ready to drink right now with a piece of juicy steak.

🛒 *Liquorland Ahuriri; Beachaven Liquor; Village Winery, Mt Eden; Liquorette Northcote; or contact Burleigh Trading for more stockists, phone (09) 480 0789.*

★★★ **2001 Tyrrell's Long Flat Vineyard Shiraz**
$15-16

It's easy to see why this wine has had a cult-like following for years. Its soft tannins and warm fruity flavours make it an instant winner as a drinking red, with or without food. It's light and fresh but beguilingly tasty in a raspberry fruity style. Good value for money.

🛒 *Widely available.*

★★½ **2001 Tyrrell's Old Winery Shiraz**
$12-13 Like many Hunter Valley shirazes, this one has an earthy aroma and flavour giving it more interest than the ubiquitous jammy taste of much Australian shiraz on the market. Above average value for money.
🍷 *Widely available.*

★★★ **2001 Tyrrell's Wines Moore's Creek Shiraz**
$13-14 It's no surprise to find this basic everyday shiraz tasting incredibly soft and way too drinkable. Australia's biggest red strength is shiraz – biggest, in terms of quantity and overall quality. And even at this price, the wine delivers layers of fruit, spice, savoury and sweet flavours. Great value.
🍷 *Glengarry, North Island.*

★★★ **2001 Wally's Hut Shiraz**
$11-12 This wine is new to New Zealand wine drinkers and it delivers good value for money with its flavours of sweet black plums, hints of sweet cherries and cedary oak that intermingle and linger in a medium-bodied style. Good value for money.
🍷 *Glengarry, North Island; or contact Marcus Pickens at Hancocks for more stockists, phone (09) 379 3740.*

★★★ **2001 Wolf Blass Red Label Shiraz Cabernet Sauvignon**
$14-15 This is a good value Australian red from one of that country's most famous wineries. This wine has layers of appeal from its juicy, shirazy taste of plums to the backbone offered by the cabernet sauvignon and the lingering tasty finish.
🍷 *Widely available.*

★★★½ 2001 Wolf Blass South Australia Shiraz
$19-20

This is the superior of the two Wolf Blass wines in this chapter, with sweeter sherbety, zingy flavours that explode in the mouth and linger long at the end of each mouthful. Great value. Buy lots.

Widely available.

★★★ 2000 Wyndham Estate Bin 555 Shiraz
$14-15

Sweet, juicy, succulent shiraz from Australia with a great price tag. This is outstanding value for money, delivering heaps of flavour.

Widely available.

★★★½ 2001 Wynns Coonawarra Estate Shiraz
$17-18

Here's a great cellaring prospect. Just two years old but this is impressively clean, complex and ripe in flavour. It is as fresh as a daisy and as juicy and tasty as a black Damson plum, just picked. Keep this stunning under-$20 red for a year or three and see it soften out or enjoy it now.

Widely available.

★★★½ 1999 Wynns Coonawarra Estate Shiraz Cabernet Merlot
$17-18

This is one of the best shirazes in this chapter, even at this incredibly youthful stage of its life. Flavours are tight and tannic at this point and consist of ripe-tasting, sweet, juicy dark plums bound up in a spicy package. With time this will open up beautifully and soften out to become a more savoury-styled creature.

Widely available.

★★★★ **1999 Yalumba Barossa Shiraz**
$19-20

Wow! This is an extremely impressive red in this price range, offering so much sweet flavour and depth and length that it is hard to believe it only costs $19.95 – or less when supermarkets special it. The grapes grown in this wine come from the Barossa Valley, spiritual home to shiraz nowadays. Fab wine!

Specialist wine stores.

★★★ **2001 Yalumba Oxford Landing Shiraz**
$12-13

This affordable little red proves that shiraz really is the grape for Aussie, offering far more flavour and value than the other wines in the Oxford Landing range. It is still light and clean and basic but has some ripe sweet fruit flavour too. Delicious grapey wine.

New World, Pak 'N Save, specialist wine stores.

★★★ **2000 Yalumba Y Shiraz**
$15-16

Stylish new mid-tier range shiraz with sherbety spiciness and plummy flavour to burn, in a tasty but unapologetically light style.

Specialist wine stores.

BUBBLIES

The most famous bubbly is Champagne, from the region of the same name in north-east France, and only sparkling wine from this area may call itself champagne, none of which makes it into this guide.

Sparkling wine is also known as asti in Italy, cava in Spain and méthode traditionelle or méthode champenoise which are used to name bubblies made in places like Australia, California and New Zealand.

Angas Brut Cuvée NV
★★★
$12-13

The first sip of this highly affordable Australian bubbly tastes like chardonnay with bubbles, but the taste of the less obvious pinot noir soon kicks in, adding length and a hint of strawberry taste to this medium to dry sparkling wine. It is great value for money.

🛒 *Specialist wine stores.*

Aquila
★★½
$8-9

Very light, aromatic bubbly in the same mould as Bernadino but ever-so-slightly drier and with a slightly longer finish. Very good value sweetish fizz for those just new to wine.

🛒 *Widely available.*

Asti Gancia
★★★½
$19-20

One sip of this will have you uttering lots of pleasant 'mmms'. It really is the most deliciously inviting style of Italian sparkling wine, made from spicy and sweet muscat but not at all cloying in taste, sweetness or flavour. Bravo to importers Phil and Ann Clark for bringing it into New Zealand last year. Great value.

🛒 *Specialist wine stores, or contact importer Phil Clark at A Touch of Italy for more information, phone (09) 273 3701, email: sales@touchofitaly.co.nz*

Bernadino Spumante
★★★½
$7-8

Lovely light, aromatic bubbly, best value sparkling wine in New Zealand, if price and flavour are the only concerns. This is an unashamedly muscat, sweetish style but not at all cloying, especially if you serve it chilled and drink it early in the afternoon or evening. Fantastic value.

🛒 *Widely available.*

★★½ **Bouvet Brut**
$19-20

A dry méthode champenoise from France. Basic quaffing bubbly that is clean and medium in body, slightly austere in style.

🛒 *Specialist wine stores, or contact Wine Direct for a store near you, or for mail order, freephone 0800 660 777.*

★★½ **Canellesi Asti Spumante Vignaioli**
$16-17

'Our challenge to Riccadonna,' says Ian Isaacs from one of New Zealand's best wine stores, Scenic Cellars on the shores of Lake Taupo. This is a lovely light muscat with typical floral and rosy, spicy and sweet flavours finishing on a medium-dry note.

🛒 *Scenic Cellars, Roberts Street, Taupo, phone (07) 378 5704, email: info@sceniccellars.co.nz*

★★ **Chardon Medium Pink Sparkling Wine**
$5-6

Pretty pink-coloured fizz with little flavour other than a hint of sweetness carried along in an innocuous style.

🛒 *Widely available.*

★★ **Chardon Medium Sparking White Wine**
$5-6

Light, sweetish white made in an attractive, slightly drier style than the pink Chardon, above. Decent value at the bottom end of the prices.

🛒 *Widely available.*

Cuvée Justine Vouvray

★★★ $19-20

This Loire Valley bubbly from France is a real style departure from most of the sparkling wines in this chapter, which tend to come from Australia and New Zealand. By contrast, here is an appley-tasting sparkling wine with a lingering finish and fresh style and also just a touch of earthiness at the start. Adventurous palates will enjoy the change.

🍷 *Chateauneuf store, 48 Pollen Street, Ponsonby, Auckland, or by mail order, phone (09) 378 7011, email: Chateauneuf@xtra.co.nz*

Diva Brut

★★½ $9-10

Innocuous dryish white bubbly with a slightly salty tang at the finish, making it a good match with nibble foods like olives, capers and spicy dips.

🍷 *Widely available.*

Diva Cuvée

★★ $9-10

Sweetish coconutty-tasting fizz with a bit of an astringent finish.

🍷 *Widely available.*

Duca di Castelmonte Le Sfere Zibbio

★★★ $16-17

Apart from the cute bottle and name, this is also an appealing-tasting Sicilian bubbly in the classic moscato Italian style. It's made from spicy sweet muscat and has a relatively high level of sweetness but finishes clean and refreshing. Serve it chilled and drink it in the sunshine.

🍷 *Specialist wine stores, or contact importer Phil Clark at A Touch of Italy for more information, phone (09) 273 3701, email: sales@touchofitaly.co.nz*

★★½ **Freixenet Cordon Negro**
$12-13

The Spanish word for sparkling wine is cava, and this one is a style departure from the bubbles we drink in this part of the world. It has fresh flavours and also a distinctive earthy, coconutty taste to it. The finish on this bubbly is lingering and this is good value for money.

Widely available.

★★★½ **Grandin Méthode Traditionelle Brut**
$19-20

This dry French bubbly smells like a bag of freshly picked apples, which is not surprising when you realise that the wine comes from the Loire Valley in central France, so is made predominantly from chenin blanc grapes, which are known for their apple-fresh crispness and vigorous acid. This is a refreshing and slightly different style of bubbly, crisp and dry.

Liquor stores, or contact Federal Geo for stockists, phone (09) 578 1823, email: federalgeo@xtra.co.nz

★★ **Hardys Sparkling**
$8-9

Good value Australian bubbly with an aromatic flavour of lightly floral grapeyness and a medium-length finish.

Widely available.

★★½ **Henkell Trocken**
$16-17

Chill this just a tad and you'll love its refreshing, crisp style and long, citrusy finish.

Liquor stores and supermarkets, or contact Federal Geo for stockists, phone (09) 578 1823, email: federalgeo@xtra.co.nz

★★ **Italiano Spumante Bianco**
$6-7 Very pretty, sweet fizzy white made from Muscat.
🛒 *Widely available.*

★★★ **Italiano Spumante Rosso**
$6-7 A lovely, lively, true Spumante style in the Italian mode. A sweetish style but very attractive and well made.
🛒 *Widely available.*

★★ **J C Le Roux La Chanson**
$14-15 Very basic sparkling white wine from South Africa with a slightly oily texture and a finish erring on the medium-sweet side.
🛒 *Selected supermarkets, or contact Burleigh Trading for more stockists, phone (09) 480 0789.*

★★ **J C Le Roux La Chanson**
$14-15 A slightly sweet, sparkling red wine from South Africa with a light body and finish. Pretty average.
🛒 *Selected supermarkets, or contact Burleigh Trading for more stockists, phone (09) 480 0789.*

★★★ **Jacob's Creek Chardonnay Pinot Noir Brut Cuvée**
$11-12 This Australian bubbly is made from the two most widely utilised grapes for champagne-making: chardonnay and pinot noir. It's a light bubbly with a zesty lemon-tasting finish and very good value for money.

🛒 *Widely available.*

Kraemer
★★★
$12-13

Crisp, light nutty and lemon flavours combine here to make this very good value for money bubbly, especially in this price range.

🧺 *Liquor stores and supermarkets, or contact Federal Geo for stockists, phone (09) 578 1823, email: federalgeo@xtra.co.nz*

KWV Mousseaux Blanc Sparkling Wine
★★★
$12-13

This is very good value sparkling wine from South Africa. It is fresh in flavour and emulates the taste of dry champagne well, albeit in a lighter style.

🧺 *Liquor stores and supermarkets, or contact Federal Geo for stockists, phone (09) 578 1823, email: federalgeo@xtra.co.nz*

Lindauer Brut
★★★½
$12-13

Lovely pinot noir-tasting bubbly with freshness and vibrant style that is consistent from bottle to bottle.

🧺 *Widely available.*

Lindauer Fraise
★★★
$13-14

Subtitled 'Lindauer & Strawberry', this is a very sweet wine that aims to pick up mainly young drinkers beguiled currently by ready-to-drink premixed spirits. It's a great marketing innovation and less than a year into its life is one of the country's biggest-selling wine brands, growing the market for wine drinkers generally. It will appeal to sweet-tooths, but wine drinkers should opt for the straight Lindauer or, better still, Lindauer Special Reserve, which has a hint of pink, plenty of pinot noir flavour and lots of value.

🧺 *Widely available.*

★★★
$12-13

Lindauer Rosé
Looks pretty and tastes pretty too, just a light, fresh, strawberry-tasting bubbly that is full of flavour in a lightish style and at this price it is fantastic value for money.
Widely available.

★★★
$12-13

Lindauer Sec
Good value Lindauer, always consistent and much sweeter (50 percent sweeter) than standard Lindauer, giving it wide appeal for new wine drinkers and those with a sweet tooth. This is very good buying.
Widely available.

SPARKLING WINE OF THE YEAR

★★★½
$15-16

STAR BUY
$15-20
BUBBLY
&
SPARKLING WINE
OF THE YEAR

Lindauer Special Reserve
This is the best-value and best-tasting sparkling wine in the book this year, flavoursome in a way that implies pinot noir's cherry tastes and robust body. It has deliciously long lingering flavours and an extremely good-value price tag. Buy heaps.
Widely available.

★★★
$12-13

2001 Lindemans Bin 25 Chardonnay Brut Cuvée
This sparkling Australian chardonnay is, as the word 'brut' on the label suggests, suitably dry to serve at night as well as during the day. It's a light style but its lemon flavours are surprisingly elegant and well balanced. The finish is short and crisp and the wine is good value for money.
Widely available.

★★★ $19-20
Luna di Luna The Original Sparkling Chardonnay Pinot Grigio

There's no missing this bright blue bottle or its rather flavoursome, beguiling contents, but a sparkling blend of chardonnay and pinot grigio (pinot gris) is definitely original only to Italy, where this bubbly comes from. I like the unusual blend of grapes in this wine, which results in an instantly appealing taste, slightly sweet at the front palate and lingering and dry at the finish. Very good value.

Specialist wine stores, or contact importer Phil Clark at A Touch of Italy for more information, phone (09) 273 3701, email: sales@touchofitaly.co.nz

★★★½ $15-16
Martini e Rossi Asti

Fantastic Italian bubbly that gains its sweetness from aromatic-tasting muscat grapes rather than anything added. It is a refreshing and delicious sparkling wine with a great price tag and – even better – just 7 percent alcohol, meaning that a couple of glasses goes down very nicely without the heady after-effects.

Widely available.

★★ $8-9
Matthew Lang Brut Cuvée Extra Dry

Australian sparkling white that makes basic drinking at best. It is slightly earthy in taste.

Widely available.

★★½ $18-19
Mills Reef Méthode NV Traditional Method

This is like chardonnay with bubbles and has a robust medium body and medium length. It's a bubbly made in the traditional style, with mid-yellow colour.

Widely available at wine stores nationwide, or contact Mills Reef Winery, phone (07) 576 8800.

Mondoro Asti

★★★
$16-17

This deliciously good Italian bubbly is widely available and consistently tasty. It errs unashamedly on the sweet side with its musky, floral and grapey flavours derived from the muscat grape from which the wine is made. It finishes on a refreshingly medium note and contains a lovely light 7.5 percent alcohol – making it very good for drinking in the sun, chilled.

🛒 *Widely available.*

Morris Sparkling Shiraz Durif

★★★
$19-20

Fantastic sparkling wine from the country that put bubbly red on the map, Australia. This is a blend of shiraz and durif grapes and, while it has a gutsy flavour, the wine itself is soft in texture and a little too easy to drink. There is a hint of black pepper intermingling with the plum fruit flavours. Great value for money.

🛒 *Specialist wine stores.*

Muscador Muscat Rosé

★★
$11-12

Very light, pretty pink wine. Basic and innocuous.

🛒 *Scenic Cellars, Roberts Street, Taupo, phone (07) 378 5704, email: info@sceniccellars.co.nz*

Nobilo Brut Pinot Noir Chardonnay

★★★
$13-14

A classy, dry New Zealand bubbly made from pinot noir and chardonnay grapes, both the most widely used grapes in Champagne, the spiritual home of sparkling wine. This is light in flavour with a crisp, dry, vaguely citrusy finish. Very elegant and good value.

🛒 *Widely available.*

★★ **Nobilo White Cloud Medium NV**
$8-9

Clean, innocuous white with a hint of light aromatic floral and raisiny flavour. Good value for new wine drinkers. Serve chilled.

🧺 *Widely available in supermarkets.*

★★★ **Nobilo White Cloud Sparkling**
$8-9

Very tasty, light and aromatic style of bubbly that tastes like biting into a big juicy muscat grape. This wine is full of sweet, spicy aromas and flavours and has a light body but lingering finish. Great value for money.

🧺 *Widely available in supermarkets.*

★★★ **Omni NV**
$12-13

Every year this wine tastes surprisingly classy, which means it is only lightly fruity and finishes with a dry and lingering finish. Fantastic value for money and elegant enough to impress the fussiest palates at a stand-up party.

🧺 *Liquor stores nationwide.*

★★★½ **2002 Pauletts Polish Hill River Sparkling Riesling**
$19-20

Trust the Australians to make something as unique as a sparkling riesling, which is relatively rare in the wine world. This wine works well as a bubbly because the riesling has been fermented to be dry in style, making it extremely refreshing as well as varietally pure, with lime and lemon flavours and a long finish. Great value for money.

🧺 *Specialist wine stores, or contact Lace Wines, phone (09) 828 4725.*

Pol Remy Pêche

★★★
$7-8

The label of this French bubbly says 'cocktail a base de vin' but the wine is apparently made from muscat grapes as well as added peach 'arome' or flavour. And it is very peachy, though strangely and refreshingly not at all cloying. Another drawcard is the low 6 percent alcohol, which means you can easily tuck away a couple of glasses and hardly notice the effect. Chill this wine down to enjoy its refreshing style. Great value for money.

🍷 *Chateauneuf store, 48 Pollen Street, Ponsonby, Auckland or by mail order, phone (09) 378 7011, email: Chateauneuf@xtra.co.nz*

Prosecco Vino Spumante Extra Dry

★★
$14-15

In its distinctive bright blue bottle, this is pretty light and dry for the style of Italian bubbly it is. I find the extra-dry flavour detracts from the already light wine, but it's not going to break the bank for a sunny picnic wine, if you want something fun and frivolous.

🍷 *Specialist wine stores, or contact importer Phil Clark at A Touch of Italy for more information, phone (09) 273 3701, email: sales@touchofitaly.co.nz*

Queen Adelaide Brut

★★½
$9-10

Light, fresh, cleansing white bubbly to drink during the day when you're looking for something light and easy on the palate.

🍷 *Widely available.*

★★½ **Robard & Butler Cuvée**
$10-11
This tasty bubbly is a consistent winner around this price – great if you can get it for a $10 note. It tastes like chardonnay with bubbles, has medium weight and even a hint of length at the end of each mouthful. Very good value fizz.
🛒 *Widely available.*

★★½ **St Aubyns Dry Sparkling Wine Black Label**
$7-8
This sweetish bubbly is fresh and clean with a hint of muscat grapeyness to it without being at all cloying. And it does finish in a crisp, dry style and it is good value for money.
🛒 *Widely available.*

★★★ **St Aubyns Medium Sparkling Wine Gold Label**
$7-8
This is the sweeter of the two St Aubyns bubblies and, although that is not necessarily always a desirable thing to be, I prefer its honest, pure, fresh muscat flavours, which are not as crisp as the Black Label but still finish on a clean, fresh note. It is not cloying but does need to be served chilled to enjoy it at its best. Great value for a muscat bubbly.
🛒 *Widely available.*

★★½ **2001 Seaview Brut**
$11-12
Basic Australian fizz for parties or daytime barbecues. Pretty average value, given its slightly earthy flavour.
🛒 *Widely available.*

Sir James Cuvée Brut

★★★　$17-18

This much-accoladed Australian bubbly sports a new label this year, but the wine inside is still made from pinot noir and chardonnay. And like previous years it is a very elegant, dry sparkling wine with a long finish.

Liquorland nationwide.

Trilogy Cuvée Brut

★★★½　$15-16

This is stunning value for money as it has those lovely dry, crisp, almost austere flavours of great champagne. And it is made, like champagne, from the chardonnay, pinot noir and pinot meunier grapes. It's zingy, concentrated without being over-the-top, and beautifully balanced with a lingering finish.

Specialist wine stores.

Verde Méthode Traditionnelle

★★★½　$17-18

This deliciously crisp, fresh bubbly tastes as if it is made predominantly from chardonnay, with its light-lemon colour and flashes of citrusy flavour. Very classy, elegant wine and great value under $20.

Widely available.

2001 Wyndham Estate S222 Sparkling Chardonnay

★★½　$14-15

This very light sparkling wine from Australia is made in a fresh style and has a medium-length finish. Clean and refreshing for daytime drinking.

Widely available.

★★ **2001 Wyndham Estate S555 Sparkling Shiraz**
$18-20 Bubbly Australian red made in the Hunter Valley, north of Sydney. This is a slightly drying red with an earthy taste. Fairly basic.
🛒 *Widely available.*

★★½ **2002 Wyndham Estate 1828 Brut Cuvée**
$9-10 This sparkling wine is called a vintage bubbly since it is made from grapes grown solely in one year, 2002. It's a light, dryish bubbly with a relatively short finish but crisp lemony flavours.
🛒 *Widely available.*

SWEET TREATS

Botrytised or late-harvested dessert wines have been made with grapes which have hung on the vines longer than usual. This results in higher sugar levels in the grapes and often also means the grapes gather botrytis rot, which shrivels them and concentrates their flavours. This means each grape has only a little, very concentrated, juice to yield for winemaking – delicious to taste but expensive to make.

Dessert wines can be made from almost any grape variety but are mostly made from aromatic white grapes such as gewürztraminer, riesling and sauvignon blanc. Italy and Spain also use red grapes to make dessert wines.

★★★ 2001 Cairnbrae Late Harvest Riesling
$19-20

This is a light style of New Zealand dessert wine with unctuous honey aromas and flavours, finishing on a green ginger note. It is tasty stuff but really comes into its own when served with sweet, creamy puddings.

Specialist wine stores, or contact Cairnbrae Vineyards, phone (03) 572 8018, email: info@cairnbrae.co.nz

★★★ 1999 Chateau Beausejour Sauvignon Sémillon Sauternes
$16-17

This French dessert wine is a nicely balanced departure from the unctuous style of many New Zealand pudding wines. It is sweet but not over-the-top and oozing honeyed flavours. Tasty wine for a light dessert.

Chateauneuf store, 48 Pollen Street, Ponsonby, Auckland, or by mail order, phone (09) 378 7011, email: Chateauneuf@xtra.co.nz

★★★ 2002 Coopers Creek Reserve Late Harvest Riesling
$19-20

This wine just begs for a delicious light pudding such as panna cotta or sorbet served with a smattering of sweet cream. It is lovely honey-tasting wine with beautiful balance and, although there is still a little bit of a gingery flavour lurking in here, it's all in good balance and good value for money too.

Most wine stores and supermarkets nationwide.

★★½ 1997 Deen De Bortoli Vat 5 Botrytis Sémillon
$14-15

If you're a fan of aged, treacly-tasting stickies, then drink this up now. It's all honey, apricots and treacle in flavour but is right in the middle of that tunnel that signals the end of this wine's life. Drink up.

Widely available.

★★★ 1998 Gramps Botrytis Sémillon
$19-20

This is deliciously developed and apricoty in flavour but ready to drink now. Find a piece of blue creamy cheese, and leave it out while you lightly chill the wine and call some friends over. Great value for money too.

🧺 *Specialist wine stores.*

★★★ 2002 Matua Valley Late Harvest Muscat
$12-13

This is an honest wine, made from grapes grown in Gisborne. Has a light-pink colour and deliciously drinkable flavour of pure Muscat-flavoured grapes with a slightly gewürzy spiciness. It transcends the rose-petal thing, leading further down the spicy path of cinnamon and nutmeg-type flavours. Fantastic stuff.

🧺 *Widely available in supermarkets and bottle stores, or contact the winery for more stockists, phone (09) 411 8301, email: sales@matua.co.nz*

★★ 2002 Nederburg Special Late Harvest
$11-12

Luscious, sweet, juicy dessert wine which tastes like an excellent food match with sticky desserts, but on its own it tastes a little short on the finish.

🧺 *Widely available.*

★★★ Pellegrino Vin Santo
$13-14

Italian grapes grillo and catarratto are used in this lovely honey-tasting Italian dessert wine. Vin Santo means, literally, holy wine and this luscious little number is perfect with a piece of good parmagiano reggiano. Lightly chill the wine and eat with a chunk of the best parmagiano you can buy.

🧺 *Specialist wine stores, or contact importer Phil Clark at A Touch of Italy for more information, phone (09) 273 3701, email: sales@touchofitaly.co.nz*

$14-15

1999 St Helena Canterbury Late Harvest
Lovely, luscious late-harvest wine with immediate appeal at the sweet front of each mouthful followed by a light-styled and slightly short finish.

Specialist wine stores, or St Helena Wines, phone (03) 323 8202.

$16-17

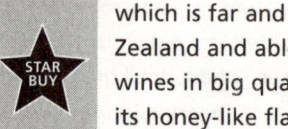

2002 Saints Gisborne Noble Sémillon
This delicious dessert wine is made by Montana Wines, which is far and away the largest winery in New Zealand and able to turn out some extremely good wines in big quantities. This is sensational sémillon with its honey-like flavours and unctuous, sticky texture. It provides great value for money and very impressive flavours, regardless of its price. If you like sweet wines, then scoop up at least half a case of this one.

Widely available.

★★★
$15-16

2001 Sandalford Element Late Harvest Riesling
This is a very fresh and dryish-styled Australian riesling made from grapes that were picked late in order to make this flavoursome little white, made to drink with dessert. It is tasty but not over-the-top and will match lemon or lime tart perfectly.

Raumati South Foodmarket; Super Liquor, Johnsonville; The Mill Liquorsave; or contact Burleigh Trading for more stockists, phone (09) 480 0789.

★★★ **2001 Seifried Estate Riesling Ice Wine**
$19-20
This wine captures everything I love about riesling in a raisin-tasting, concentrated style, and it will be a winner with dessert-wine-lovers every time it is opened. It's a class act, oozing lots of unctuous characters but still manages to taste clean and fresh without being cloying. Great value for money for this sort of delicious little number.
♛ *Widely available.*

★★★ **2002 Selaks Marlborough Ice Wine**
$14-15
Delicious pudding wine with intense sweet stewed apple and custard tastes in a light- to medium-bodied style with a lingering finish. Good value.
♛ *Widely available.*

★★★ **2002 Waimea Estate Late Harvest Riesling**
$15-16
This is a light rather than luscious pudding wine, made to drink now with fresh fruit or something simple and refreshing – try it with lime sorbet, a winning combination.
♛ *Liquor King, Liquorland, most supermarkets.*

★½ **Wohnsiedler Sauternes**
$6-7
Innocuous, inoffensive stuff with a hint of acid helping to balance this very sweet but very light style. Just drinkable.
♛ *Widely available.*

SHERRY AND SHERRY-STYLED FORTIFIED WINES

Sherry comes in two main styles: pale fino sherry and dark oloroso sherry. Variations resulting from these two main stylistic themes include manzanilla, fino, amontillado, oloroso, pale cream and cream. Another is Pedro Ximenez (often abbreviated to PX on bottles), an extremely concentrated sweet fortified wine.

Three grape varieties are planted in modern-day vineyards in Jerez: palomino (the most important), pedro ximenez and muscat of Alexandria.

The name sherry is an English adaptation of the Spanish word Jerez – Jerez de la Frontera is a city in the Andalucia region in the south of Spain and is the home of sherry.

Anything called 'sherry' coming from anywhere outside of Spain is an imitation of the real thing, which, like champagne, can only come from the soil, climate and place of origin.

Cellarmans Amontillado Sherry

★★★
$10-11

A very good look-alike for the real thing. This wine sports a lovely sharp, tangy bite of that salty, seaside character that Spanish sherry has. It's just a shame it is still called 'sherry', which should really be the privilege reserved for those wines that come from Jerez; the namesake of 'sherry'.

Liquor stores and specialist wine stores.

Cellarmans Extra Special Sherry

★★½
$11-12

There are plenty of people who will find this sherry extra special but it tastes to me mostly of a kick of hot alcohol at the finish and a caramel, woody taste in the mid-palate. Still, it's easy-to-enjoy quaffing sherry, best served chilled on ice to cut down the hot finish.

Liquor stores and specialist wine stores.

Cellarmans Oloroso Medium Sweet Sherry

★½
$10-11

A bit dirty and bland, very oxidized, which does nothing to aid the overtly sweet flavour of this wine.

Liquor stores and specialist wine stores.

Cellarmans Select Rich Cream Sherry

★★½
$8-9

Mid-golden colour with a very light aroma of burnt peaches and a sweetish, enjoyable mid-palate that finishes drier than the extra special version above, making this one far more special.

Liquor stores and specialist wine stores.

★★ **Ormond Rich Cream**
$8-9
Light, sweet-tasting and, yes, creamy in texture. It finishes short at the end of each mouthful and delivers value if you have a sweet tooth.
Liquor stores and specialist wine stores.

★★★ **Pykes Cream Sherry**
$11-12
Lovely golden brown-orange colour with classic medium-styled port flavours of orange peel and spice. Yum! Great with spiced nuts and aromatic nibbles.
Liquor stores and specialist wine stores.

★★★ **Pykes Fino Sherry**
$11-12
Light fino with a slight tang and a hint of earthy savoury flavour too. Fantastic value for money and it is the real thing – from Spain.
Liquor stores and specialist wine stores.

★★★ **Pykes Medium Sherry**
$11-12
Strong creamy, woody character in this wine, making it great value for money. Lovely pure, medium-dry finish.
Liquor stores and specialist wine stores.

STAR BUY

PORT, MARSALA AND PORT LOOK-ALIKES, AND FORTIFIED WINES

If it is not from Portugal, it's not port, but fortified wines can be made in a similar style. Like many European wines, port takes its name from where it comes from – Oporto, which is the second biggest city in Portugal and one of the most interesting historic places to explore in that most western country in Europe. Only fortified wines made in Oporto may use the name 'port', although many other countries have in the past used the word 'port' to describe their fortified wine.

Port can be made from more than 80 different grape varieties, but the most popular grapes used in it are touriga nacional, tinta barroca, touriga francesa, tinta roriz and tinto cao.

Countries outside Portugal have made wine they've called 'port' using any and many other grape varieties.

★★½ Cellarmans Hallmark Ruby Port
$10-11
Light and insubstantial in the mouth but the slightly woody tang on the finish adds character to this cheap and relatively cheerful fortified wine, which is made from grapes grown in Australia and New Zealand – so it should be called fortified wine.
Liquor stores and specialist wine stores.

★★★ Cromwell Renmano Tawny Port
$12-13
This is pure brown sugar in flavour with a touch of alcohol, adding zest and zing to its sweet finish. Good, basic porty-tasting fortified wine.
Liquor stores nationwide.

★★★ Hardys Tall Ships Port
$16-17
This is like liquefied dried fruit and nuts held together in a steamy fortified wine. It will easily woo lovers of ports and other fortified reds because of its sweet flavours and dryish finish. Since it is made from grapes grown in Australia, however, this is not port – despite the label – but rather a fortified wine.
Widely available.

★★★ Morris Rutherglen Liqueur Muscat
$19-20
This sweet fortified Australian muscat is great value for money, particularly given the glorious bottle and packaging (yes, fantastic gift). It has spicy flavours which remind me of orange, clove and almonds, and while it tastes good with all those flavours this is even better with a creamy soft blue cheese or even poured over a light ice cream.
Specialist wine stores.

Morris Rutherglen Liqueur Tawny Port

★★★ $19-20

If you have been on a long search for a wine that tastes great with chocolate, then your quest has come to an end. This deeply golden-coloured fortified wine from Australia is perfect with chocolate as its flavours taste like caramel, brown sugar and warm stewed fruit.

Specialist wine stores.

Morris Rutherglen Liqueur Tokay

★★★ $19-20

Like the liqueur muscat in this range, this tokay is also good with chocolate, with its tasty cinnamon, nutmeg and brown-sugar flavours.

Specialist wine stores.

Orlando Liqueur Port

★★ $18-20

This is a light, aromatic Australian fortified liqueur with tastes of sweet brown sugar and caramalised peaches.

Specialist wine stores.

Ormond Rich Ruby

★½ $8-9

At least it's not called port because it bears no resemblance to even cheap versions of the real thing. This is sweet all the way through with very little wine taste at all. It is difficult to complain about the price but as far as value for money goes, this is average.

Liquor stores and specialist wine stores.

★★★
$17–18

Pellegrino Dom De Marsala

This big sister to the Marsala Superiore (below) is a noticeable step up in quality with all those delicious burnt orange, clove, cinnamon and nutmeg flavours held together in a zingier wine with higher acids, balancing out the sweetness and adding length of flavour. Excellent value.

🛒 *Specialist wine stores, or contact importer Phil Clark at A Touch of Italy for more information, phone (09) 273 3701, email: sales@touchofitaly.co.nz*

★★½
$12–13

Pellegrino Garibaldi Marsala Superiore

This lovely Italian marsala has classic burnt orange flavours with light spicy tastes of cloves and cinnamon in a delicious mix. Fantastic value for money as either an after-dinner drink or for use in extra-special desserts. Try it as a base for bread and butter pudding matched with this wine – magic.

🛒 *Specialist wine stores, or contact importer Phil Clark at A Touch of Italy for more information, phone (09) 273 3701, email: sales@touchofitaly.co.nz*

★★½
$19–20

Pykes Fine Ruby

Sweet, raisins and spicy nutmeg flavours with a short finish; not quite as good in quality as the tawny but easily approachable for those with a sweet tooth.

🛒 *Liquor stores and specialist wine stores.*

★★★
$19–20

Pykes Fine Tawny

Sharp, sweet, piquant flavours and sweet, fruity raisin tastes make this a tasty non-vintage, everyday entry-level port. Fantastic value for money at this price and quality level.

🛒 *Liquor stores and specialist wine stores.*

★★★
$10-11

Robard & Butler Artillery Port
Now this is more like it – a spicy, robust, lovely port look-alike – although it's not port! Yes, I'm still banging that drum, because the Australians should have stopped using the word 'port' years ago and this is 'product of Australia'. Still, it is a quality wine, especially for just $10–11, which is hard-to-beat value.
 Widely available.

ACKNOWLEDGEMENTS

Writing a thank-you list is a nerve-wracking task when all other writers say they leave someone vitally important off their thank-you list. Those who assisted with this book supplied wine for assessment, provided information and took the time to read previous editions of the book in order to offer suggestions for improvements and alterations.

Comments are listened to and taken on board. Many are reflected in this book while others may take a little longer to be effected. I hope I have not forgotten to thank anybody in the following list but, if I have, my apologies and thanks for your support and encouragement.

Thank you to all of the wineries and wine importers who provided wine for this year's edition of *Joëlle Thomson's Under $20 Wine Guide*, keeping my doorstep, office and kitchen bench piled high with wine for tasting.

Thank you also for ongoing support, samples and information to: Montana Wines, Orlando Wyndham, Villa Maria, Nobilo Wines, BRL Hardy, Hancocks, Bennett & Deller Wine Merchants, Wineworks Solutions, Wine Direct, Federal Geo, Vintage Wines & Spirits, Eurowine, Negociants, Seifried Estate, Morton Estate, Beringer Blass, Cellier le Brun, Lincoln Vineyards, Kim Crawford Wines, West Brook Wines, Odyssey Wines, Vavasour, Wine Masters, Matariki Wines, Saint Clair Estate, Torlesse Wines, Scenic Cellars, Forrest Estate, Linden Estate, Cross Roads Winery, Burleigh Trading, Soljans Estate, Collards Wines, de Gyffarde Wines, Worldwide Wines, Alan McCorkindale Wines, Waipara West, Waipara Springs, Wine Masters, Sacred Hill, Crab Farm Winery, Mission Estate, Matua Valley, Giesen, Southcorp Wines, Tasman Bay Wines, Wairau River Wines, Okahu Estate, Trinity Hill, Domaine Georges Michel, Clifford Bay Estate and all the other New Zealand wineries who quietly entered wine for tasting for this book.

Thanks to Caro's Wines who allowed us to do the cover photo shoot at their premises.

Thank you to writers and colleagues Vic Williams and Peter Saunders for their insight, encouraging words and constructive suggestions for future editions of this guide.

Thank you to Peter Barker and Ruby Barker-Thomson and to my agent Glenys Bean.

Joëlle Thomson